Readings in Literary Criticism 22

CRITICS ON POE

Readings in Literary Criticism

1. CRITICS ON KEATS
2. CRITICS ON CHARLOTTE AND EMILY BRONTË
3. CRITICS ON POPE
4. CRITICS ON MARLOWE
5. CRITICS ON JANE AUSTEN
6. CRITICS ON CHAUCER
7. CRITICS ON BLAKE
8. CRITICS ON VIRGINIA WOOLF
9. CRITICS ON D. H. LAWRENCE
10. CRITICS ON YEATS
11. CRITICS ON DRYDEN
12. CRITICS ON MELVILLE
13. CRITICS ON WHITMAN
14. CRITICS ON EMILY DICKINSON
15. CRITICS ON EZRA POUND
16. CRITICS ON HAWTHORNE
17. CRITICS ON ROBERT LOWELL
18. CRITICS ON HENRY JAMES
19. CRITICS ON WALLACE STEVENS
20. CRITICS ON EMERSON
21. CRITICS ON MARK TWAIN
22. CRITICS ON POE

Readings in Literary Criticism

1. CRITICS ON KEATS
2. CRITICS ON CHARLOTTE AND EMILY BRONTË
3. CRITICS ON POPE
4. CRITICS ON MARLOWE
5. CRITICS ON JANE AUSTEN
6. CRITICS ON CHAUCER
7. CRITICS ON BLAKE
8. CRITICS ON VIRGINIA WOOLF
9. CRITICS ON D. H. LAWRENCE
10. CRITICS ON YEATS
11. CRITICS ON DRYDEN
12. CRITICS ON MELVILLE
13. CRITICS ON WHITMAN
14. CRITICS ON EMILY DICKINSON
15. CRITICS ON EZRA POUND
16. CRITICS ON HAWTHORNE
17. CRITICS ON ROBERT LOWELL
18. CRITICS ON HENRY JAMES
19. CRITICS ON WALLACE STEVENS
20. CRITICS ON EMERSON
21. CRITICS ON MARK TWAIN
22. CRITICS ON POE

Readings in Literary Criticism 22

CRITICS ON POE

CRITICS ON POE

Readings in Literary Criticism
Edited by David B. Kesterson

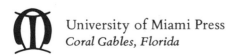

University of Miami Press
Coral Gables, Florida

Library of Congress Cataloging in Publication Data

Kesterson, David B   1938-   comp.
    Critics on Poe

    (Readings in literary criticism, 22)
    1. Poe, Edgar Allan, 1809-1849. I. Title.
PS2638.K44   818' .3'09   73-77554
ISBN 0-87024-252-0

CONTENTS

ACKNOWLEDGMENTS   7

INTRODUCTION   9

TABLE OF IMPORTANT DATES   11

CRITICS ON POE: 1845-1940   13

Margaret Fuller, James Russell Lowell, Rufus W. Griswold,
Evert A. Duyckinck, Charles Beaudelaire, Sarah Helen
Whitman, A. C. Swinburne, Henry James, Thomas Wentworth
Higginson, E. C. Stedman, Walt Whitman, William Dean
Howells, R. H. Stoddard, Vernon L. Parrington, Aldous
Huxley, Una Pope-Hennessy

CRITICS ON POE SINCE 1940   42

Arthur H. Quinn, Van Wyck Brooks, Howard Mumford Jones,
T. S. Eliot, Allen Tate, N. B. Fagin, Edward H. Davidson,
Vincent Buranelli, Edward Wagenknecht, Robert D. Jacobs

GENERAL CRITICAL EVALUATIONS

JAMES W. GARGANO
The Question of Poe's Narrators   56

BRANDER MATTHEWS
Poe and the Detective Story   63

CONSTANCE ROURKE
Humor in Poe   70

EDMUND WILSON
Poe as a Literary Critic   74

FLOYD STOVALL
The Achievement of Poe   79

CRITICS ON SPECIFIC WORKS

ROY P. BASLER
The Interpretation of "Ligeia"   85

WILLIAM BYSSHE STEIN
The Twin Motif in "The Fall of the House of Usher"   96

JOSEPH PATRICK ROPPOLO
Meaning and "The Masque of the Red Death"   98

6   CONTENTS

E. ARTHUR ROBINSON
Poe's "The Tell-Tale Heart"   107
EDWARD H. DAVIDSON
The Meaning of "The Raven"   115
KATHRYN M. HARRIS
Ironic Revenge in Poe's "The Cask of Amontillado"   121

SELECTED BIBLIOGRAPHY   125

ACKNOWLEDGMENTS

Roy P. Basler: from "The Interpretation of 'Ligeia,' " *College English*, Vol. 5 (1944). Copyright held by the author. Reprinted by permission of the author.

Van Wyck Brooks: from the book, *The World of Washington Irving*, by Van Wyck Brooks. Copyright 1944, 1950 by Van Wyck Brooks. Everyman's Library Edition. Published by E. P. Dutton & Co., Inc. and used with their permission.

Vincent Buranelli: from *Edgar Allan Poe* by Vincent Buranelli, published by Twayne Publishers, Inc. Copyright 1961 by Twayne Publishers, Inc. Reprinted by permission of the publisher.

Edward H. Davidson: reprinted by permission of the publishers from pp. 84-92 of Edward H. Davison, *Poe: A Critical Study*. Cambridge, Mass.: The Belknap Press of Harvard University Press, copyright 1957 by the President and Fellows of Harvard College.

T. S. Eliot: from *To Criticize the Critic* by T. S. Eliot, copyright 1948 by Thomas Stearns Eliot, copyright © 1965 by Valerie Eliot. Reprinted with the permission of Farrar, Straus & Giroux, Inc. and Faber and Faber Ltd.

N. B. Fagin: from "Edgar Allan Poe," *South Atlantic Quarterly*, Vol. 51 (1952), 279-80. Reprinted by permission of Duke University Press.

James W. Gargano: from "The Question of Poe's Narrators," *College English*, Vol. 25 (1963). Copyright © 1963 by the National Council of Teachers of English. Reprinted by permission of the publisher and the author.

Kathryn M. Harris: from "Ironic Revenge in Poe's 'The Cask of Amontillado,' " *Studies in Short Fiction*, Vol. 6 (1969). Reprinted by permission of the author and the publisher.

Aldous Huxley: from *Vulgarity in Literature: Digressions from a Theme*, published by Harper & Row, Inc. and by Chatto and Windus Ltd. Reprinted by permission of Mrs. Laura Huxley, Harper & Row, Inc., and Chatto and Windus Ltd.

Lois and Francis F. Hyslop, Jr.: from *Baudelaire on Poe* published by Bald Eagle Press. Reprinted by permission of the publisher.

Robert D. Jacobs: from *Poe: Journalist and Critic* published by Louisiana State University Press. Reprinted by permission of the publisher.

Howard Mumford Jones: from *Ideas in America* published by Harvard University Press. Reprinted by permission of the publishers.

Vernon L. Parrington: from *The Romantic Revolution in America* by Vernon L. Parrington, copyright 1927 by Harcourt Brace Javanovich, Inc.; renewed 1954 by Vernon L. Parrington, Jr., Louise P. Tucker, and Elizabeth P. Thomas. Reprinted by permission of the publishers.

Una Pope-Hennessy: from *Edgar Allan Poe* by Una Pope-Hennessy, published by Macmillan, London and Basingstoke. Reprinted by permission of Macmillan, London and Basingstoke.

Arthur H. Quinn: from *Edgar Allan Poe* published by Cooper Square Publishers, Inc. Reprinted by permission of the publisher.

E. Arthur Robinson: from "Poe's 'The Tell-Tale Heart,' " © 1965 by The Regents of the University of California. Reprinted from *Nineteenth Century Fiction,*

Vol. 19, No. 4, pp. 369-378 by permission of The Regents and the author.

Joseph P. Roppolo: from "Meaning and 'The Masque of the Red Death,' " *Tulane Studies in English,* Vol. 13 (1963), 59-69. Reprinted by permission of the author.

Constance Rourke: from *American Humor* by Constance Rourke, copyright 1931 by Harcourt Brace Jovanovich, Inc.; renewed 1959 by Alice D. Fore. Reprinted by permission of the publishers.

William Bysshe Stein: from "The Twin Motif in 'The Fall of the House of Usher,' " *Modern Language Notes,* Vol. 75 (1960), 109-111. © The Johns Hopkins University Press. Reprinted by permission of The Johns Hopkins University Press.

Floyd Stovall: from Introduction to *The Poems of Edgar Allan Poe* by Floyd Stovall, published by The University Press of Virginia. Reprinted by permission of the publisher.

Allen Tate: from *Essays of Four Decades,* published by The Swallow Press, Chicago, Copyright 1968 by Allen Tate. Reprinted by permission of the author and The Swallow Press.

Edward Wagenknecht: from *Edgar Allan Poe: The Man Behind the Legend* by Edward Wagenknecht. Copyright © 1963 by Edward Wagenknecht. Reprinted by permission of Oxford University Press, Inc.

Edmund Wilson: from "Poe as a Literary Critic," *The Nation,* Vol. 155 (1942), pp. 452-53. Reprinted by permission of the publisher.

INTRODUCTION

EDGAR ALLAN POE has been a critical anomaly since his own day. Critics have praised him, loathed him, apologized for him. They have called him a first-rate writer of genius and a charlatan appealing to popular taste. Alfred, Lord Tennyson believed that Poe was America's most original genius. Emerson, on the other hand, labeled him a "jingle man." William Butler Yeats proclaimed Poe a great lyric poet. Henry James and William Dean Howells found little of merit in him for the mature mind. The French impressionists, on whom Poe asserted a major influence, loved him. Even in attempting to determine Poe's primary contribution to literature there is major disagreement. Poe is all poet to some, all craftsman of short fiction to others, all critic and aesthetic theoretician to another group, mainly an influence on literature to still others. Whatever the critical reaction to Poe, however, one truth is quite apparent: no one has been able to ignore him.

Nineteenth-century dissent over Poe began as a reaction to the man personally. Poe's personal reputation suffered immediately after his death because of the smear tactics of Rufus Wilmot Griswold, Poe's literary executor and author of the infamous "Ludwig" obituary in 1849. Griswold spitefully depicted Poe as a blackguard and a ne'er-do-well, a friendless egotist who was a "brilliant, but erratic" literary star. It took the work of many pens—among them those of early defenders John Ingram and Sarah Helen Whitman—to set aright the image. But there was another factor in misreading Poe's personality in the nineteenth century, and that was the man himself. Moody, theatrical, hard-working, yet frequently unpredictable and inconsistent in his behavior as well as in his ideas and literary criticism, Poe spawned an image of instability that misled many critics who were overly anxious to pinpoint salient character traits. Indeed, Poe enjoyed posing; images gave the more sensitive Poe shields to hide behind. But the images caused him to be misunderstood.

Poe's contemporaries also found fault with his works. They attacked him for the apparent lack of moral concern in his writings and for his exotic flights of fancy. Martin Tupper called the works immoral and fantastic. Walt Whitman, while recognizing Poe's lyrical genius, regretted that the works were "without the first sign of moral principles." The art for art's sake people welcomed Poe's poetry, but those who deemed the moral tradition necessary to poetry, who believed art should be the handmaiden of philosophy, or who preferred art to be more bourgeois in subject and appeal disparaged his efforts.

Yet his century was also quick to recognize his genius, and Poe had many advocates during his lifetime and afterward. Critics extolled his vivid creative imagination and admired the technical beauty of his works. Bluestocking Margaret Fuller found Poe's writings refreshing, calling them "the fruit of genuine observations and experience, combined with an invention that is not 'making-up.' " James Russell Lowell, an astute critic himself, praised Poe's critical powers and admired his early poetry. Across the Atlantic Baudelaire described Poe as an admirable idealist fighting a battle with the materialism of his age. Dostoevsky singled out the realistic detail, perceptive insights, and rich imagination evident in Poe's works.

Twentieth-century criticism has continued to explain, defend, or denigrate Poe but has generally responded more favorably to him than critics before 1900. In the first half of the century, two major biographies—by Joseph Wood Krutch (1926) and Arthur Hobson Quinn (1941)—sought to establish and reconsider the facts of Poe's life in light of twentieth-century distance and understanding. Krutch's book evinces the psychological—in particular the Freudian—interest in Poe that has become a mainstay in Poe criticism. Quinn's emphasis is on biographical facts in an attempt to present the whole man and get away from legend. Since mid-century, scholars have been less prone to dwell on Poe's personal life and questionable reputation and have concentrated on his talents, contributions, or his life in relation to his work, with major books such as Edward Davidson's interpretative study (1957) and Edward Wagenknecht's exploration of the "man behind the legend" (1963) being outstanding examples of this trend. New views of Poe as critic, Poe as journalist, Poe as poet, Poe involved in his social-business sphere, Poe as literary influence have been in vogue since the late fifties, the sixties especially bringing forth innumerable reevaluative and reinterpretive books and articles. Poe's achievements are at long last fully recognized and proficiently presented and explained in what amounts to a spate of recent criticism.

The selections in the first two parts of this volume survey the criticism on Poe since 1845. Especially noteworthy are the "Ludwig" article and reactions to Poe by famous nineteenth-century persons of several nationalities. The third part offers more detailed reactions to Poe's art and accomplishments, reflecting the growing tendency among twentieth-century critics to concentrate on specific topics inherent in Poe's art. From the general literary historian, Russell Blankenship, to the specialist in Poe, Floyd Stovall, Poe's endeavors in all literary fields are surveyed and evaluated. The final portion of the book focuses on a selection of Poe's chief works and presents some of the most distinguished twentieth-century criticism on these works. The essays stand as reminders of how advanced Poe criticism has become since 1845.

North Texas State University, 1973   DAVID B. KESTERSON

TABLE OF IMPORTANT DATES

1809	Edgar Poe was born in Boston, January 19, to Elizabeth Arnold Poe and David Poe, Jr.
1811	Poe's mother died in Richmond. Poe taken in by John Allan family and christened Edgar Allan Poe.
1815	Poe went to England with the Allans; attended Manor House School (1817-1820).
1820	Returned to Richmond with the Allans.
1825	Became engaged to Sarah Elmira Royster.
1826	Entered the University of Virginia.
1827	Engagement with Sarah Royster broken; left the University, quarreled with John Allan, enlisted in U.S. Army (under the alias "Edgar A. Perry"), and published *Tamerlane and Other Poems.*
1829	Discharged from the army after the death of Mrs. Allan. Published *Al Aaraaf, Tamerlane and Minor Poems.*
1830	Entered West Point.
1831	Expelled from West Point. Went to New York to live and then on to Baltimore. Published *Poems.*
1832	Lived in obscurity. Published five tales, "Metzengerstein" being the most important.
1833	Awarded a fifty-dollar prize by the Baltimore *Saturday Visitor* for story, "Ms. Found in a Bottle."
1834	John Allan died March 27. Poe not mentioned in his will.
1835	In December assumed editorship of the *Southern Literary Messenger.* Published "Berenice," "Morella," and "Hans Pfaal."
1836	Married Virginia Clemm, his thirteen-year-old cousin.
1837	Resigned editorship on *Southern Literary Messenger* and went to New York.
1838	In New York published *Narrative of Arthur Gordon Pym.* "Ligeia" appeared after Poe moved to Philadelphia.
1839	Became editor of Burton's *Gentleman's Magazine* from May 1839 to June 1840. *Tales of the Grotesque and Arabesque* appeared in December, containing the famous "Fall of the House of Usher."

1840   Left *Gentleman's Magazine.* Released his own plans for a journal, "Prospectus for *The Penn Magazine,*" but failed to get support for the project.

1841   Editor of *Graham's Magazine* in April. Published "The Murders in the Rue Morgue" and "A Descent into the Maelstrom."

1842   Left *Graham's.* Published short stories and the famous review of Hawthorne's *Twice-Told Tales.* Virginia became ill.

1843   "The Gold Bug" received a hundred-dollar prize from the Philadelphia *Dollar Newspaper.* Other publications: "The Pit and the Pendulum," "The Tell-Tale Heart," and "The Black Cat."

1844   Back to New York in April with ailing Virginia and Mrs. Clemm. Wrote for *Sunday Times* and later New York *Evening Mirror.* Several stories published.

1845   "The Raven" published January 29 in *Evening Mirror.* Poe gained wide recognition. Became editor of the *Broadway Journal.* Published *Tales* and *The Raven and Other Poems.*

1846   *Broadway Journal* collapsed financially in January. Poe moved to a cottage in Fordham with his wife and Mrs. Clemm. Publications included "The Cask of Amontillado" and "The Philosophy of Composition."

1847   Virginia died in January. Poe despondent. Published "The Domain of Arnheim" and "Ulalume."

1848   Engaged briefly to Mrs. Sarah Helen Whitman, a widow. Gave his famous lecture "The Poetic Principle" in Lowell, Massachusetts, and published *Eureka.*

1849   Published "For Annie," "Eldorado," "Annabel Lee," and "The Bells." Had romances with Mrs. Richmond and Mrs. Shelton (Sarah Elmira Royster). Died in a Baltimore hospital on October 7.

Critics on Poe: 1845-1940

MARGARET FULLER: 1845

Poe's Tales

MR. POE'S TALES need no aid of newspaper comment to give them popularity; they have secured it. We are glad to see them given to the public in this neat form, so that thousands more may be entertained by them without injury to their eyesight.

No form of literary activity has so terribly degenerated among us as the tale. Now that everybody who wants a new hat or bonnet takes this way to earn one from the magazines or annuals, we are inundated with the very flimsiest fabrics ever spun by mortal brain. Almost every person of feeling or fancy could supply a few agreeable and natural narratives, but when instead of using their materials spontaneously they set to work with geography in hand to find unexplored nooks of wild scenery in which to locate their Indians or interesting farmers' daughters, or with some abridgment of history to hunt monarchs or heroes yet unused to become the subjects of their crude coloring, the sale-work produced is a sad affair indeed and "gluts the market" to the sorrow both of buyers and lookers-on.

In such a state of things the writings of Mr. Poe are a refreshment, for they are the fruit of genuine observations and experience, combined with an invention which is not "making up," as children call their way of contriving stories, but a penetration into the causes of things which leads to original but credible results. His narrative proceeds with vigor, his colors are applied with discrimination, and where the effects are fantastic they are not unmeaningly so.

The "Murders in the Rue Morgue" especially made a great impression upon those who did not know its author and were not familiar with his mode of treatment. Several of his stories make us wish he would enter the higher walk of the metaphysical novel and, taking a mind of the self-possessed and deeply marked sort that suits him, give us a deeper and longer acquaintance with its life and the springs of its life than is possible in the compass of these tales.

As Mr. Poe is a professed critic and of all the band the most unsparing to others, we are surprised to find some inaccuracies in the use of words, such as these: "he had with him many books, but rarely *employed* them."—"His results have, in truth, the *whole air* of intuition."

The degree of skill shown in the management of revolting or terrible circumstances makes the pieces that have such subjects more interesting than the others. Even the failures are those of an intellect of strong fiber and well-chosen aim.

From the New York *Daily Tribune,* 11 July 1845, p. 1.

JAMES RUSSELL LOWELL: 1845

Poe's Genius

MR. POE is at once the most discriminating, philosophical, and fearless critic upon imaginative works who has written in America. It may be that we should qualify our remark a little, and say that he *might be*, rather than that he always *is*, for he seems sometimes to mistake his phial of prussic-acid for his inkstand. If we do not always agree with him in his premises, we are, at least, satisfied that his deductions are logical, and that we are reading the thoughts of a man who thinks for himself, and says what he thinks, and knows well what he is talking about. His analytic power would furnish forth bravely some score of ordinary critics. We do not know him personally, but we suspect him for a man who has one or two pet prejudices on which he prides himself. These sometimes allure him out of the strict path of criticism, but, where they do not interfere, we would put almost entire confidence in his judgments. Had Mr. Poe had the control of a magazine of his own, in which to display his critical abilities, he would have been as autocratic, ere this, in America, as Professor Wilson has been in England; and his criticisms, we are sure, would have been far more profound and philosophical than those of the Scotsman. As it is, he has squared out blocks enough to build an enduring pyramid, but has left them lying carelessly and unclaimed in many different quarries. . . .

Mr. Poe's early productions show that he could see through the verse to the spirit beneath, and that he already had a feeling that all the life and grace of the one must depend on and be modulated by the will of the other. We call them the most remarkable boyish poems that we have ever read. We know of none that can compare with them for maturity of purpose, and a nice understanding of the effects of language and metre. Such pieces are only valuable when they display what we can only express by the contradictory phrase of *innate experience*. . . .

Mr. Poe has two of the prime qualities of genius, a faculty of vigorous yet minute analysis, and a wonderful fecundity of imagination. The first of these faculties is as needful to the artist in words, as a knowledge of anatomy is to the artist in colors or in stone. This enables him to conceive truly, to maintain a proper relation of parts, and to draw a correct outline, while the second groups, fills up, and colors. Both of these Mr. Poe has displayed with singular distinctness in his prose works, the last predominating in his earlier tales, and the first in his later ones. In judging of the merit of an author, and assigning him his niche among our household gods, we have a right to regard him from our own point of view, and to measure him by our own standard. But, in estimating his works, we must be governed by his own design, and, placing them by the side of his own ideal, find how much is wanting. We differ with Mr. Poe in his opinions of the objects of art. He esteems that object to be the creation of Beauty, and perhaps it is only in the definition of that word that we disagree with him. But in what we shall say of his writings we shall take his own standard as our guide. The temple of the god of song is equally accessible from every side, and there is room enough in it for all who bring offerings, or seek an oracle.

In his tales, Mr. Poe has chosen to exhibit his power chiefly in that dim region which stretches from the very utmost limits of the probable into the weird confines of superstition and unreality. He combines in a very remarkable manner two faculties which are seldom found united; a power of influencing the mind of the reader by the impalpable shadows of mystery, and a minuteness of detail which does not leave a pin or a button unnoticed. Both are, in truth, the natural results of the predominating quality of his mind, to which we have before alluded, analysis. It is this which distinguishes the artist. . . .

This analyzing tendency of his mind balances the poetical, and, by giving him the patience to be minute, enables him to throw a wonderful reality into his most unread fancies. A monomania he paints with great power. He loves to dissect these cancers of the mind and to trace all the subtle ramifications of its roots.

Beside the merit of conception, Mr. Poe's writings have also that of form. His style is highly finished, graceful and truly classical. It would be hard to find a living author who had displayed such varied powers. As an example of his style we would refer to one of his tales, "The House of Usher," in the first volume of his "Tales of the Grotesque and Arabesque." It has a singular charm for us, and we think that no one could read it without being strongly moved by its serene and sombre beauty. Had its author written nothing else it would alone have been enough to stamp him as a man of genius, and the master of a classic style. . . .

Mr. Poe is still in the prime of life, being about thirty-two years of age, and has probably as yet given but an earnest of his powers. As a critic, he has shown so superior an ability that we cannot but hope that he will collect his essays of this kind and give them a more durable form. They would be a very valuable contribution to our literature, and would fully justify all we have said in his praise. We could refer to many others of his poems than those we have quoted, to prove that he is the possessor of a pure and original vein. His tales and essays have equally shown him a master in prose. It is not for us to assign him his definite rank among contemporary authors, but we may be allowed to say that we know of *none* who has displayed more varied and striking abilities.

From "Edgar Allan Poe," *Graham's Magazine,* 27 (1845), 49-53.

RUFUS WILMOT GRISWOLD: 1849

The "Ludwig" Article

EDGAR ALLAN POE is dead. He died in Baltimore the day before yesterday. This announcement will startle many, *but few will be grieved by it.* The poet was well known personally or by reputation, in all this country; he had readers in England, and in several of the states of Continental Europe; *but he had few or no friends;* and the regrets for his death will be suggested principally by the consideration that in him literary art lost one of its most brilliant, but erratic, stars.

The family of Mr. Poe, we learn from Griswold's "Poets and Poetry of America," from which a considerable portion of the facts in this notice are derived, was one of the oldest and most respectable in Baltimore. David Poe, his paternal grandfather, was a Quartermaster-General in the Maryland line during the Revolution, and the intimate friend of Lafayette, who during his last visit to the United States, called personally upon the General's widow, and tendered her acknowledgments for the services rendered to him by her husband. His great-grandfather, John Poe, married in England, Jane, a daughter of Admiral James McBride, noted in British naval history, and claiming kindred with some of the most illustrious English families. His father and mother,—both of whom were in some way connected with the theatre, and lived as precariously as their more gifted, and more eminent son,— died within a few weeks of each other, of consumption, leaving him an orphan at two years of age. Mr. John Allan, a wealthy gentleman of Richmond, took a fancy to him, and persuaded his grandfather to suffer him to adopt him. He was brought up in Mr. Allan's family, and as that gentleman had no other children, he was regarded as his son and heir. In 1816 he accompanied Mr. and Mrs. Allan to Great Britain, visited every portion of it, and afterward passed four or five years in a school kept at [Stoke] Newington, near London, by Rev. Dr. Bransby. He returned to America in 1822, and in 1825 went to the Jefferson University, at Charlottesville, in Virginia, where he led a very dissipated life, the manners of the College at that time being extremely dissolute. He took the first honors, however, and went home greatly in debt. Mr. Allan refused to pay some of his debts of *honor,* and he hastily quitted the country on a quixotic expedition to join the Greeks, then struggling for liberty. He did not reach his original destination, however, but made his way to St. Petersburg, in Russia, when he became involved in difficulties, from which he was extricated by the late Henry Middleton, the American Minister at that Capital. He returned home in 1829, and immediately afterwards entered the Military Academy at West Point. In about eighteen months from that time, Mr. Allan, who had lost his first wife while Mr. Poe was in Russia, married again. He was sixty-five years of age, and the lady was young; Poe quarreled with her, and the veteran husband, taking the part of his wife, addressed him an angry letter, which was answered in the same spirit. He died soon after, leaving an infant son heir to his property, and bequeathing Poe nothing.

The army, in the opinion of the young poet, was not a place for a poor man; so he left West Point abruptly, and determined to maintain himself by authorship. He printed, in 1827, a small volume of poems, most of which were written in early youth. Some of these poems are quoted in a review by Margaret Fuller, in *The Tribune* in 1846, and are justly regarded as among the most wonderful exhibitions of the precocious developments of genius. They illustrated the character of his abilities, and justified his anticipations of success. For a considerable time, however, though he wrote readily and brilliantly, his contributions to the journals attracted little attention, and his hopes of gaining a livelihood by the profession of literature was nearly ended at length in sickness, poverty and despair.

But in 1831 [1833], the proprietor of a weekly gazette, in Baltimore, offered two premiums, one for the best story in prose, and the other for the best poem.

In due time Poe sent in two articles, and he waited anxiously for the decision. One of the Committee was the accomplished author of "Horseshoe Robinson," John P. Kennedy, and his associates were scarcely less eminent than he for wit and critical sagacity. Such matters were usually disposed of in a very offhand way; committees to award literary prizes drink to the payer's health, in good wines, over the unexamined MSS., which they submit to the discretion of the publisher, with permission to use their names in such a way as to promote the publisher's advantage. So it would have been in this case, but that one of the Committee, taking up a small book, in such exquisite calligraphy as to seem like one of the finest issues of the press of Putnam, was tempted to read several pages, and being interested, he summonsed [sic] the attention of the company to the half-dozen compositions in the volume. It was unanimously decided that the prizes should be paid to the first of geniuses who had written legibly. Not another MS. was unfolded. Immediately the confidential envelope was opened, and the successful competitor was found to bear the scarcely known name of Poe.

The next day the publisher called to see Mr. Kennedy, and gave him an account of the author that excited his curiosity and sympathy, and caused him to request that he should be brought to his office. Accord-

ingly he was introduced; the prize money had not yet been paid, and he
was in the costume in which he had answered the advertisement of his
good fortune. Thin, and pale even to ghastliness, his whole appearance
indicated sickness and the utmost destitution. A tattered frock-coat
concealed the absence of a shirt, and the ruins of boots disclosed more
than the want of stockings. But the eyes of the young man were luminous with intelligence and feeling, and his voice and conversation, and
manners, all won upon the lawyer's regard. Poe told his history, and his
ambitions, and it was determined that he should not want means for a
suitable appearance in society, nor opportunity for a just display of his
abilities in literature. Mr. Kennedy accompanied him to a clothing
store, and purchased for him a respectable suit, with changes of linen,
and sent him to a bath, from which he returned with the suddenly
regained bearing of a gentleman.

The late Mr. Thomas W. White had then recently established *The
Southern Literary Messenger,* at Richmond, and upon the warm recom-
mendation of Mr. Kennedy, Poe was engaged at a small salary—we
believe of $500 a year—to be its editor. He entered upon his duties with
letters full of expression of the warmest gratitude to his friends in
Baltimore, who in five or six weeks were astonished to learn that with
characteristic recklessness of consequence, he was hurriedly married to
a girl as *poor as himself.* Poe continued in this situation for about a year
and a half, in which he wrote many brilliant articles, and raised the
Messenger to the first rank of literary periodicals.

He next removed to Philadelphia, to assist William E. Burton in the
editorship of the *Gentleman's Magazine,* a miscellany that in 1840 was
merged in *Graham's Magazine,* of which Poe became one of the princi-
pal writers, particularly in criticism, in which his papers attracted much
attention by their careful and skilful analysis, and general caustic sever-
ity. At this period, however, he appeared to have been more ambitious
of securing distinction in romantic fiction, and a collection of his compositions in this department, published in 1841, under the title of Tales
of the Grotesque and the Arabesque, established his reputation for ingenuity, imagination, and extraordinary power in tragical narration.

Near the end of 1844 Poe removed to New York, where he con-
ducted for several months a literary miscellany called the *Broadway
Journal.* In 1845 he published a volume of "Tales" in Wiley and Putnam's "Library of American Books"; and in the same series a collection
of his poems. Besides these poems he was the author of "Arthur Gordon Pym," a romance; "Eureka," an essay on the spiritual and material
universe, a work which he wishes to have "judged as a poem"; and
several extended series of papers in the periodicals, the most noteworthy of which are "Marginalia," embracing opinions of books and
authors; "Secret Writing," "Autography"; and "Sketches of the Literati
of New York."

His wife died in 1847, at Fordham, near this city, and some of our readers will remember the paragraphs in the papers of the time, upon his destitute condition. We remember that Col. Webb collected in a few moments fifty or sixty dollars for him at the Metropolitan Club; Mr. Lewis, of Brooklyn, sent a similar sum from one of the courts, in which he was engaged when he saw the statement of the poet's poverty; and others illustrated in the same manner the effect of such an appeal to the popular heart.

Since that time Mr. Poe had lived quietly, and with an income from his literary labors sufficient for his support. A few weeks ago he proceeded to Richmond, in Virginia, where he lectured upon the poetical character, etc.; and it was understood by some of his correspondents here that he was this week to be married, most advantageously, to a lady of that city, a widow, to whom he had been previously engaged while a student in the University.

The character of Mr. Poe we cannot attempt to describe in this very hastily written article. We can but allude to some of the more striking phases.

His conversation was at times almost supramortal in its eloquence. His voice was modulated with astonishing skill, and his large and variably expressive eyes looked reposed or shot fiery tumult into theirs who listened, while his own face glowed or was changeless in pallor, as his imagination quickened his blood, or drew it back frozen to his heart. His imagery was from the worlds which no mortal can see but with the vision of genius. Suddenly starting from a proposition exactly and sharply defined in terms of utmost simplicity and clearness, he rejected the forms of customary logic, and in a crystalline process of accretion, built up his ocular demonstrations in forms of gloomiest and ghostliest grandeur, or in those of the most airy and delicious beauty, so minutely, and so distinctly, yet so rapidly, that the attention which was yielded to him was chained till it stood among his wonderful creations—till he himself dissolved the spell, and brought his hearers back to common and base existence, by vulgar fancies or by exhibitions of the ignoble passions.

He was at times a dreamer—dwelling in ideal realms—in heaven or hell, peopled with creations and the accidents of his brain. He walked the streets, in madness or melancholy, with lips moving in indistinct curses, or with eyes upturned in passionate prayers (never for himself, for he felt, or professed to feel, that he was already damned), but for their happiness who at that moment were objects of his idolatry; or with his glance introverted to a heart gnawed with anguish, and with a face shrouded in gloom, he would brave the wildest storms; and all night, with drenched garments and arms wildly beating the wind and rain, he would speak as if to spirits that at such times only could be evoked by him from that Aidenn close by whose portals his disturbed

soul sought to forget the ills to which his constitution subjected him—
close by that Aidenn where were those he loved—the Aidenn which he
might never see but in fitful glimpses, as its gates opened to receive the
less fiery and more happy natures whose listing to sin did not involve
the doom of death. He seemed, except when some fitful pursuit subjected his will and engrossed his faculties, always to bear the memory of
some controlling sorrow. The remarkable poem of *The Raven* was probably much more nearly than has been supposed, even by those who
were very intimate with him, a reflection and an echo of his own
history. He was the bird's

> —unhappy master,
> Whom unmerciful disaster
> Followed fast and followed faster
> Till his song the burden bore—
> Melancholy burden bore
> Of "Nevermore," of "Nevermore."

Every genuine author in a greater or less degree leaves in his works,
whatever their design, traces of his personal character; elements of his
immortal being, in which the individual survives the person. While we
read the pages of the *Fall of the House of Usher,* or of *Mesmeric
Revelation,* we see in the solemn and stately gloom which invests one,
and in the subtle metaphysical analysis of both, indications of the
idiosyncrasies,—of what was most peculiar—in the author's intellectual
nature. But we see here only the better phases of this nature, only the
symbols of his juster action, for his harsh experience had deprived him
of all faith in man or woman.

He had made up his mind upon the numberless complexities of the
social world, and the whole system was with him an imposture. This
conviction gave a direction to his shrewd and naturally unamiable character. Still though he regarded society as composed of villians, the
sharpness of his intellect was not of that kind which enabled him to
cope with villainy, while it continually caused him overshots, to fail of
the success of honesty. He was in many respects like Francis Vivian in
Bulwer's novel of the "Caxtons." "Passion, in him, comprehended
many of the worst emotions which militate against human happiness.
You could not contradict him, but you raised quick choler; you could
not speak of wealth, but his cheek paled with gnawing envy. The astonishing natural advantage of this poor boy—his beauty, his readiness, the
daring spirit that breathed around him like a fiery atmosphere—had
raised his constitutional self-confidence into an arrogance that turned
his very claims to admiration into prejudice against him. Irascible,
envious—bad enough, but not the worst, for these salient angles were all
varnished over with a cold repellant cynicism while his passions vented

themselves in sneers. There seemed to him no moral susceptibility; and what was more remarkable in a proud nature, little or nothing of the true point of honor. He had, to a morbid excess, that desire to rise which is vulgarly called ambition, but no wish for the esteem or the love of his species; only the hard wish to succeed—not shine, not serve—succeed, that he might have the right to despise a world which galled his self-conceit."

We have suggested the influence of his aims and vicissitudes upon his literature. It was more conspicuous in his later than his earlier writing. Nearly all that he wrote in the last two or three years—including much of his best poetry—was in some sense biographical; in draperies of his imagination, those who had taken the trouble to trace his steps, could perceive, but slightly covered, the figure of himself. . . .

We must omit any particular criticism of Mr. Poe's works. As a writer of tales it will be admitted generally, that he was scarcely surpassed in ingenuity of construction or effective painting; as a critic, he was more remarkable as a dissector of sentences than as a commenter upon ideas. *He was little better than a carping grammarian.* As a poet, he will retain a most honorable rank. Of his "Raven," Mr. Willis observes, that in his opinion, "it is the most effective single example of fugitive poetry ever published in this country, and is unsurpassed in English poetry for subtle conceptions, masterly ingenuity of versification, and consistent sustaining of imaginative lift." In poetry, as in prose, he was most successful in the metaphysical treatment of the passions. His poems are constructed with wonderful ingenuity, and finished with consummate art. They illustrate a morbid sensitiveness of feeling, a shadowy and gloomy imagination, and a taste almost faultless in the apprehension of that sort of beauty most agreeable to his temper.

We have not learned the circumstance of his death. It was sudden, and from the fact that it occurred in Baltimore, it is presumed that he was on his return to New York.

"After life's fitful fever he sleeps well."

—Ludwig

From "Death of Edgar A. Poe," New York *Daily Tribune,* 9 October 1849, p. 2.

EVERT A. DUYCKINCK: 1850

"A Man of Ideas"

POE WAS strictly impersonal; as greatly so as any man whose acquaintance we have enjoyed. In a knowledge of him extending through several years, and frequent opportunities, we can scarcely remember to have had from him any single disclosure or trait of personal character; anything which marked him as a mover or observer among men. Although he had travelled in distant countries, sojourned in cities of our own country, and had, at different times, under favorable opportunities, been brought into contact with life and character of many phases, he had no anecdote to tell, no description of objects, dress, or appearance. Nothing, in a word, to say of things. Briefly, he was what Napoleon named an ideologist—a man of ideas. He lived entirely apart from the solidities and realities of life: was an abstraction; thought, wrote, and dealt solely in abstractions. It is this which gives their peculiar feature to his writings. They have no color, but are in pure outline, delicately and accurately drawn, but altogether without the glow and pulse of humanity. His genius was mathematical, rather than pictorial or poetical. He demonstrates instead of painting. Selecting some quaint and abstruse theme, he proceeds to unfold it with the closeness, care, and demonstrative method of Euclid; and you have, to change the illustration, fireworks for fire; the appearance of water for water; and a great shadow in the place of an actual, moist, and thunder-bearing sky. His indifference to living, flesh and blood subjects, explains his fondness for the mechanism and music of verse, without reference to the thought or feeling. He is therefore a greater favorite with scholars than with the people; and would be (as a matter of course) eagerly followed by a train of poetastering imitators, who, to do them justice in a familiar image, "hear the bell ring and don't know where the clapper hangs." Poe is an object of considerable, or more than considerable size; but the imitation of Poe is a shadow indescribably small and attenuated. We can get along, for a while, on a diet of common air—but the exhausted receiver of the air-pump is another thing! The method and management of many of Mr. Poe's tales and poems are admirable, exhibiting a wonderful ingenuity, and completely proving him master of the weapon he had chosen for his use. He lacks reality, imagination, every-day power, but he is remarkably subtle, acute, and earnest in his own way. His instrument is neither an organ nor a harp; he is neither a King David nor a

Beethoven, but rather a Campanologian, a Swiss bell-ringer, who from little contrivances of his own, with an ingeniously-devised hammer, strikes a sharp melody, which has all that is delightful and affecting, that is attainable without a soul.

From "Poe's Works," *The Literary World,* 6 (1850), 81.

CHARLES BAUDELAIRE: 1852

"An Antithesis Come to Life"

IF POE attracted a great deal of attention, he also made many enemies. Firm in his convictions, he made indefatigable war upon false reasoning, silly imitations, solecisms, barbarisms, and all the literary offenses perpetrated every day in newspapers and books. In these respects no fault could be found with him, for he practiced what he preached; his style is pure, adequate to his ideas and expresses them exactly. Poe is always correct. It is a very remarkable fact that a man with such a bold and roving imagination should be at the same time so fond of rules and capable of careful analyses and patient research. He might be called an antithesis come to life. His ability as a critic did much to harm his literary fortune. Many people sought revenge. They spared no pains in hurling reproaches at him as his literary production increased. Everyone is familiar with the long, banal litany: immorality, lack of feeling, lack of conclusions, absurdity, useless literature. Never has French criticism pardoned Balzac for *le Grand homme de province á Paris.*

As a poet, Edgar Poe is a man apart. Almost by himself he represents the romantic movement on the other side of the Atlantic. He is the first American who, properly speaking, has made his style a tool. His poetry, profound and plaintive, is nevertheless carefully wrought, pure, correct, and as brilliant as a crystal jewel. It is obvious that, in spite of astonishing merits, which have made them the idols of weak and sentimental souls, Alfred de Musset and Alphonse de Lamartine would not have been included among Poe's friends, had he lived among us. They lack will power and are not sufficiently masters of themselves. Edgar Poe loved complicated rhythms and, however complicated they were, they contained a profound harmony. . . .

As a novelist and storyteller, Edgar Poe is unique in his fields, as were Maturin, Balzac, and Hoffmann in theirs. The different stories which he scattered through the reviews have been gathered together in two collections, one, *Tales of the Grotesque and Arabesque,* the other, *Edgar A. Poe's Tales,* edited by Wiley and Putnam. In all they comprise a total of nearly seventy-two pieces. They contain violent buffoonery, the pure grotesque, passionate aspirations toward the infinite, and a great interest in magnetism. The small edition of short stories was as successful in Paris as in America, because it contains very dramatic things, but a most unusual form of the dramatic.

I wish I could characterize the literature of Poe very briefly and very categorically, for it is a quite new literature. What gives it its essential character and distinguishes it among all others is, if I may use these strange words, conjecturism and probabilism.

From "Edgar Allan Poe: His Life and His Works" in *Baudelaire on Poe,* ed. Lois and Francis F. Hyslop, Jr. (State College, Pa.: Bald Eagle Press, 1952), pp. 66-69; originally in *Revue de Paris,* 1852.

SARAH HELEN WHITMAN: 1860

An Answer to Griswold

IT IS NOT our purpose at present specially to review Dr. Griswold's numerous misrepresentations, and misstatements. Some of the more injurious of these anecdotes were disproved, during the life of Dr. Griswold, in the *New York Tribune* and other leading journals, without eliciting from him any public statement in explanation or apology. Quite recently we have had, through the columns of the *Home Journal,* the refutation of another calumnious story, which for ten years has been going the rounds of the English and American periodicals. . . .

It is not to be questioned that Poe was a consummate master of language—that he had sounded all the secrets of rhythm—that he understood and availed himself of all its resources; the balance and poise of syllables—the alternations of emphasis and cadence—of vowel-sounds and consonants—and all the metrical sweetness of "phrase and metaphrase." Yet this consummate art was in him united with a rare simplicity. He was the most genuine of enthusiasts, as we think we shall presently show. His genius would follow no leadings but those of his own imperial intellect. With all his vast mental resources he could never write an occasional poem, or adapt himself to the taste of a popular audience. His graver narratives and fantasies are often related with an earnest simplicity, solemnity, and apparent fidelity, attributable, not so much to a deliberate artistic purpose, as to that power of vivid and intense conception that made his dreams realities, and his life a dream. . . .

The thought which informs so many of his tales and poems betrays its sad sincerity even in his critical writings, as, for instance, in a notice of *Undine* in the "Marginalia." Yet it has been said of him that "he had no touch of human feeling or of human pity," that "he loved no one but himself"—that "he was an abnormal and monstrous creation,"— "possessed by legions of devils." The most injurious epithets have been heaped upon his name and the most improbable and calumnious stories recorded as veritable histories. Ten years have passed since his death, and while the popular interest in his writings and the popular estimate of his genius increase from year to year, these acknowledged calumnies are still going the round of the foreign periodicals and are still being republished at home.

We believe that with the exception of Mr. Willis's generous tributes to his memory, some candid and friendly articles by the Editor of the *Literary Messenger,* and an eloquent and vigorous article in *Russell's Magazine* by Mr. J. Wood Davidson, of Columbia, S.C. (who has appreciated his genius and his sorrow more justly perhaps than any of his American critics) this great and acknowledged wrong to the dead has been permitted to pass without public rebuke or protest.

In the memoir prefixed to the *Illustrated Poems,* it is said of him that "his religion was a worship of the beautiful," which is emphatically true, and that "he knew no beauty but that which is purely sensuous," which is, as emphatically, untrue. We appeal from this last assertion to Mr. Poe's own exposition of his poetic theory. He recognises the elements of poetic emotion—the emotion of the beautiful—*"in all noble thoughts, in all holy impulses, in all chivalrous, generous, and self-sacrificing deeds."* His "aesthetic religion," which has been so strangely misapprehended was simply a recognition of the divine and inseparable harmonies of the supremely Beautiful and the supremely Good.

From *Edgar Poe and His Critics* (New York: Rudd and Carleton, 1860; reissued New Brunswick: Rutgers Univ. Press, 1949), pp. 32-33, 54, 67-68.

A. C. SWINBURNE: 1875

Letter to Madam Rice: In Praise of Poe

SARA S. RICE—Dear Madam: I have heard, with much pleasure, of the memorial at length raised to your illustrious fellow-citizen.

The genius of Edgar Poe has won, on this side of the Atlantic, such wide and warm recognition that the sympathy, which I cannot hope fitly or fully to express, in adequate words, is undoubtedly shared at this moment by hundreds, as far as the news may have spread throughout not England only but France as well; where, as I need not remind you, the most beautiful and durable of monuments has been reared to the genius of Poe, by the laborious devotion of a genius equal and akin to his own; and where the admirable translation of his prose works,—by a fellow poet whom also we have to lament before his time—is even now being perfected by a careful and exquisite version of his poems, with illustrations full of the subtle and tragic force of fancy which impelled and molded the original song: a double homage, due to the loyal and loving cooperation of one of the most remarkable younger poets and one of the most powerful leading painters in France—M. Mallarmé and M. Manet.

It is not for me to offer any tribute here to the fame of your great countryman, or dilate, with superfluous and intrusive admiration, on the special quality of his strong and delicate genius,—so sure of aim, and faultless of touch, in all the better and finer part of work he has left us.

I would only—in conveying to the members of the Poe Memorial Committee my sincere acknowledgment of the honor they have done me, in recalling my name on such an occasion,—take leave to express my firm conviction that widely as the fame of Poe has already spread, and deeply as it is already rooted, in Europe, it is even now growing wider and striking deeper as time advances; the surest presage that time, the eternal enemy of small and shallow reputations, will prove in this case also the constant and trusty friend and keeper of a true poet's fullgrown fame. I remain, dear Madam, yours very truly,

A. C. Swinburne.

Printed in New York *Daily Tribune,* 27 November 1875, p. 4.

HENRY JAMES: 1876

"The Greater Charlatan"

WITH ALL due respect to the very original genius of the author of the
'Tales of Mystery,' it seems to us that to take him with more than a
certain degree of seriousness is to lack seriousness one's self. An enthusiasm for Poe is the mark of a decidedly primitive stage of reflection.
Baudelaire thought him a profound philosopher, the neglect of whose
golden utterances stamped his native land with infamy. Nevertheless,
Poe was vastly the greater charlatan of the two, as well as the greater
genius.

From "Charles Baudelaire," *The Nation,* 22 (1876), 280.

HENRY JAMES: 1879

Pioneer American Critic of Genius

THERE WAS but little literary criticism in the United States at the time Hawthorne's earlier works were published; but among the reviewers Edgar Poe perhaps held the scales the highest. He, at any rate, rattled them loudest, and pretended, more than any one else, to conduct the weighing-process on scientific principles. Very remarkable was this process of Edgar Poe's, and very extraordinary were his principles; but he had the advantage of being a man of genius, and his intelligence was frequently great. His collection of critical sketches of the American writers flourishing in what M. Taine would call his *milieu* and *moment,* is very curious and interesting reading, and it has one quality which ought to keep it from ever being completely forgotten. It is probably the most complete and exquisite specimen of *provincialism* ever prepared for the edification of men. Poe's judgments are pretentious, spiteful, vulgar; but they contain a great deal of sense and discrimination as well, and here and there, sometimes at frequent intervals, we find a phrase of happy insight imbedded in a patch of the most fatuous pedantry. He wrote a chapter upon Hawthorne, and spoke of him, on the whole, very kindly; and his estimate is of sufficient value to make it noticeable that he should express lively disapproval of the large part allotted to allegory in his tales—in defence of which, he says, "however, or for whatever object employed, there is scarcely one respectable word to be said. . . . The deepest emotion," he goes on, "aroused within us by the happiest allegory *as* allegory, is a very, *very* imperfectly satisfied sense of the writer's ingenuity in overcoming a difficulty we should have preferred his not having attempted to overcome. . . . One thing is clear, that if allegory ever establishes a fact, it is by dint of overturning a fiction."

From *Hawthorne* (New York: Harper & Brothers, 1879), pp. 62-63.

THOMAS WENTWORTH HIGGINSON: 1879

Poe's Place in Imaginative Literature

POE'S PLACE in purely imaginative prose-writing is as unquestionable as Hawthorne's. He even succeeded, which Hawthorne did not, in penetrating the artistic indifference of the French mind; and it was a substantial triumph, when we consider that Baudelaire put himself or his friends to the trouble of translating even the prolonged platitudes of "Eureka," and the wearisome narrative of "Arthur Gordon Pym." Neither Poe nor Hawthorne has ever been fully recognized in England; and yet no Englishman of our time, except possibly De Quincey, has done any prose imaginative work to be named with theirs. But in comparing Poe with Hawthorne, we see that the genius of the latter has hands and feet as well as wings, so that all his work is solid as masonry, while Poe's is broken and disfigured by all sorts of inequalities and imitation and stucco; he not disdaining, for want of true integrity, to disguise and falsify, to claim knowledge that he did not possess, to invent quotations and references, and even, as Griswold showed, to manipulate and exaggerate puffs of himself. I remember the chagrin with which I looked through Tieck, in my student-days, to find the "Journey into the Blue Distance" to which Poe refers in the "House of Usher;" and how one of the poet's intimates laughed me to scorn for being deceived by any of Poe's citations; saying that he hardly knew a word of German.

But making all possible deductions, how wonderful remains the power of Poe's imaginative tales, and how immense is the ingenuity of his puzzles and disentanglements. The conundrums of Wilkie Collins never renew their interest after the answer is known; but Poe's can be read again and again. It is where spiritual depths are to be touched that he shows his weakness; where he attempts it, as in "William Wilson," it seems exceptional; where there is the greatest display of philosophic form he is often most trivial, whereas Hawthorne is often profoundest when he has disarmed you by his simplicity. The truth is that Poe lavished on things comparatively superficial those great intellectual resources which Hawthorne reverently husbanded and used. That there is something behind even genius to make or mar it, this is the lesson of the two lives.

From "Poe," *The Literary World,* 10 (1879), 89.

E. C. STEDMAN: 1880

Poe's Enigmatic Reputation

IN THE OPINION of some people, even now, his life was not only pitiful, but odious, and his writings are false and insincere. They speak of his morbid genius, his unjust criticisms, his weakness and ingratitude, and scarcely can endure the mention of his name. Others recount his history as that of a sensitive, gifted being, most sorely beset and environed, who was tried beyond his strength and prematurely yielded, but still uttered not a few undying strains. As a new generation has arisen, and those of his own who knew him are passing away, the latter class of his reviewers seems to outnumber the former. A chorus of indiscriminate praise has grown so loud as really to be an ill omen for his fame; yet on the whole, the wisest modern estimate of his character and writings has not lessened the interest long ago felt in them at home and abroad. . . .

His intellectual strength and rarest imagination are to be found in his *Tales*. To them, and to literary criticism, his main labors were devoted.

His imagination was not of the highest order, for he never dared to trust to it implicitly; certainly not in his poetry, since he could do nothing with a measure like blank verse, which is barren in the hands of a mere songster, but the glory of English metrical forms when employed by one commanding the strength of diction, the beauty and grandeur of thought, and all the resources of a strongly imaginative poet. Neither in verse nor in prose did he cut loose from his minor devices, and for results of sublimity and awe he always depends upon that which is grotesque or out of nature. Beauty of the fantastic or grotesque is not the highest beauty. Art, like nature, must be fantastic, not in her frequent, but in her exceptional moods. The rarest ideal dwells in a realm beyond that which fascinates us by its strangeness or terror, and the votaries of the latter have masters above them as high as Raphael is above Doré.

From *Poets of America* (Boston: Houghton, Mifflin, 1894), pp. 226, 252, 258. First appeared in *Scribner's Monthly* for May 1880.

WALT WHITMAN: 1880

Poe's Significance

ALMOST WITHOUT the first sign of moral principle, or of the concrete or its heroisms, or the simpler affections of the heart, Poe's verses illustrate an intense faculty for technical and abstract beauty, with the rhyming art to excess, an incorrigible propensity toward nocturnal themes, a demoniac undertone behind every page—and, by final judgment, probably belong among the electric lights of imaginative literature, brilliant and dazzling, but with no heat. There is an indescribable magnetism about the poet's life and reminiscences, as well as the poems. To one who could work out their subtle retracing and retrospect, the latter would make a close tally no doubt between the author's birth and antecedents, his childhood and youth, his physique, his so-call'd education, his studies and associates, the literary and social Baltimore, Richmond, Philadelphia and New York of those times—not only the places and circumstances in themselves, but often, very often, in a strange spurning of, and reaction from them all.

From *Specimen Days* (entry for 1 January 1880) in *The Complete Writings of Walt Whitman* (New York: Putnam, 1902), IV, 285-86.

WILLIAM DEAN HOWELLS: 1901

"Our Great Original"?

WHAT POE DID was to enlarge our earth and sky by giving us, through the rifts he made in either, glimpses of the preternatural which have a perennial glamour; but the influence of his art, which once so thrilled and fascinated, is no longer felt in our literature. Yet if one comes to naming of names, his must be almost the first, as one perceives with a certain sense of hardship, suspecting as one does something essentially voluntary, not to say mechanical, in his witchery.

There are traces of Bryant before Bryant, as there are after him, in our poetry, but none of Poe. The nature-worship runs all through it; but the supernature-worship begins and ends with a sole hierophant. Was he then our great original; and was he this by virtue of something derived from his environment here, derivable by no other American, or was he ours rather by the accident of his birth in our quarter of a world where he had nowhere his like or fellow?

The great New Englanders would none of him. Emerson called him "the jingle-man;" Lowell thought him "three-fourths sheer fudge"; Longfellow's generous voice was silenced by Poe's atrocious misbehavior to him, and we can only infer his slight esteem for his work; in a later generation Mr. James speaks of Poe's "very valueless verses." Yet is it perversely possible that his name will lead all the rest when our immortals are duly marshalled for the long descent of time. He belongs, like the poets mentioned, to the golden age of our still youthful rhyme, which Whittier, Holmes, Taylor, Stoddard and Walt Whitman belonged to, and which Mr. Stedman classifies as our second lyrical period. Bryant, who in greatness belongs there with them, is chronologically assigned to the first lyrical period, where he has no compeer, as none of those named quite have, in the third lyrical period, or the fourth, which Mr. Stedman generalizes as "The Close of the Century."

From "A Hundred Years of American Verse," *The North American Review,* 172 (1901), 152-53.

R. H. STODDARD: 1903

The Curious Talents of Poe

HIS INVENTION was boundless, his execution limited, scanty, and sparse. He repeated himself thrice in his lines "To F. S. O.," and bettered them each time. It was the same with his stories, which he repeated many times, over and under many pen names. This strange fact was known to his foes, and his friends, who conceded it, his friends being his worst foes, and his worst foes the kindest of his few friends. Let me say here that "The Bells" was sold thrice, and paid for every time; that "Annabel Lee" was sold twice, and was printed by Griswold before it could appear either in *Sartain's Magazine* or in the *Southern Literary Messenger,* and when it possessed no literary value whatever. . . .

Oblivious of what I may have said, but fully conscious of what I mean to say, Poe was a curious compound of the charlatan and the courtly gentleman; a mixture of Count Cagliostro, of Paracelsus, who was wisely named Bombastes, and of Cornelius Agrippa,—the three beings intermoulded from the dust of Apollonius of Tyana and Elymas the Sorcerer. His first master in verse was Byron, in prose Charles Brockden Brown, and later Hawthorne.

Most men are egoists; he was egotistical. His early poems are exquisite, his later ones are simply melodious madness. The parent of "Annabel Lee" was Mother Goose, who in this instance did *not* drop a golden egg. Always a plagiarist, he was always original. Like Molière, whom he derided, he took his own wherever he found it. Without dramatic instinct, he persuaded himself (but no one else) that he was a dramatist. The proof of this assertion is his drama of "Politian," which was never ended, and which should never have been begun.

From "Meetings With Poe," *Recollections: Personal and Literary* (New York: Barnes, 1903), pp. 153-56.

VERNON L. PARRINGTON: 1927

"Outside the Main Current"

AN AESTHETE and a craftsman, the first American writer to be concerned with beauty alone, his ideals ran counter to every major interest of the New England renaissance: the mystical, optimistic element in transcendentalism; the social conscience that would make the world over in accordance with French idealism, and that meddled with its neighbor's affairs in applying its equalitarianism to the negro; the pervasive moralism that would accept no other criteria by which to judge life and letters—these things could not fail to irritate a nature too easily ruffled. The Yankee parochialisms rubbed across his Virginia parochialisms; and when to these was added a Yankee preëmption of the field of literary criticism, when a little clique engaged in the business of mutual admiration puffed New England mediocrities at his expense, the provocation was enough to arouse in a sensitive southern mind an antagonism that rivaled Beverley Tucker's. In his unhappy pilgrimage through life Poe was his own worst enemy, but he took comfort in charging his ill fortune upon the malignancy of others. . . .

So much only need be said. The problem of Poe, fascinating as it is, lies quite outside the main current of American thought, and it may be left with the psychologist and the belletrist with whom it belongs. It is for abnormal psychology to explain his "neural instability amounting almost to a dissociated or split personality," his irritable pride, his quarrelsomeness, his unhappy persecution complex, his absurd pretentions to a learning he did not possess, his deliberate fabrications about his life and methods of work, his oscillations between abstinence and dissipation, between the morbidly grotesque and the lucidly rational, his haunting fear of insanity that drove him to demonstrate his sanity by pursuing complex problems of ratiocination. Such problems are personal to Poe and do not concern us here. And it is for the belletrist to evaluate his theory and practice of art: his debt to Coleridge and Schlegel; the influence of the contemporary magazine on his conception of the length of a work of the imagination; the value of his theory of the tyrannizing unity of mood in the poem and short story; the provocation to the craftsman of the pretentiousness of contemporary American literature, joined to a flabby and crude technique; the grossness of the popular taste and the validity of his critical judgments. Whatever may be the final verdict it is clear that as an aesthete and a craftsman he made a stir in the world that has not lessened in the years since his death, but has steadily widened. Others of greater repute in his day have fared less prosperously in later reputation. He was the first of our artists and the first of our critics; and the surprising thing is that such a man should have made his appearance in an America given over to hostile ideals. He suffered much from his aloofness, but he gained much also. In the midst of gross and tawdry romanticisms he refused to be swallowed up, but went his own way, a rebel in the cause of beauty, discovering in consequence a finer romanticism than was before known in America.

From *The Romantic Revolution in America 1800-1860* (New York: Harcourt, Brace, 1927), pp. 57-59.

ALDOUS HUXLEY: 1930

Vulgarity in Poe

THE SUBSTANCE of Poe is refined; it is his form that is vulgar. He is, as it were, one of Nature's Gentlemen, unhappily cursed with incorrigible bad taste. To the most sensitive and high-souled man in the world we should find it hard to forgive, shall we say, the wearing of a diamond ring on every finger. Poe does the equivalent of this in his poetry; we notice the solecism and shudder. Foreign observers do not notice it; they detect only the native gentlemanliness in the poetical intention, not the vulgarity in the details of execution. To them, we seem perversely and quite incomprehensibly unjust.

From *Vulgarity in Literature: Digressions From a Theme* (London: Chatto and Windus, 1930), p. 27.

UNA POPE-HENNESSY: 1934

Poe and Coleridge

IN CONSIDERING the work of Poe and the conditions under which much of it was produced we are inevitably drawn to compare the action of his mind, though not its quality nor its content, with that of his first master, Coleridge. We find the same tastes, the same wide miscellaneous intake of reading material, the same interest in narratives of old sea voyages and explorations of unknown continents, the same attraction to exotic plants and tropical animals; we find further the same play of creative energy upon the assembled images and facts gathered by the mind, the same transfiguration of discourse into poetry—into poems or prose-poems; in fine, the same divine power. That Poe produced nothing so unique and dazzlingly original as *Kubla Khan* may indicate that the combustion of the heterogeneous fuel thrown into his mind took place at a lower temperature or that with him the assimilation of the raw material was less complete; and yet the work of no literary man more aptly illustrates the dictum of Coleridge, "Other men's worlds are the poet's chaos."

From *Edgar Allan Poe, 1809-1849: A Critical Biography* (London: Macmillan, 1934), pp. 323-24.

Critics on Poe since 1940

Critics on Poe since 1940

ARTHUR H. QUINN: 1941

Poe, a Man of "Lofty Standards"

OF EVEN more significance than Poe the man is Poe the artist. To bring to Virginia the few comforts she needed, he might harness his critical pen to drive a poetess, who could pay him, into temporary fame. But even the spectre of want could not force him into the prostitution of his genius as a poet and a writer of romance. Had he chosen to fill his pages with the sentimental twaddle then so popular or to sully his creations of the beautiful with the suggestiveness that sells, he would have made a better living, and would now be forgotten. But he had his own lofty standards, and he lived up to them. For money he cared little, except as it provided for the wants of others. For fame he did care, but he was one of those souls who can see a prize, artistic, social, or financial, almost within their grasp, and caring for something higher still, of which that prize is the price, can resolutely put it by. We can imagine him saying with Browning's Duke,

> "That would have taken some stooping—and I
>   choose
> Never to stoop."

It is for this great refusal, for his willingness to lay all things upon the altar of his art, that Poe is most to be respected. He could hardly have done otherwise. A patrician to the fingertips, the carefulness of his dress, even in his poverty, was but an index to his devotion to those fields of effort in which he knew he was a master. After creating the detective story, he left it to others, who could not write the Arabesques of which he alone knew the secret. Limited as his field in poetry seems at first glance to be, it deals with great universal motives, with love, beauty, pride and death, and he carried those themes into lyric heights untouched before his time in America.

In his fiction, as well as his poetry, the pioneering spirit of the America of his day showed clearly in that restlessness which led him to dream "dreams no mortal ever dared to dream before," to test the outer limits of the human soul, and to attack even the citadel of the spirit's integrity, and the relations of God and His Universe.

His fame is now secure. The America in which he could find no adequate reward treasures every word he wrote, and in every city in which he lived, except the city of his birth, stands a lasting memorial to him. He has become a world artist and through the translations of his writings he speaks today to every civilized country. He has won this wide recognition by no persistent clamor of a cult, but by the royal right of preeminence. For today, nearly a hundred years since his death, he remains not only the one American, but also the one writer in the English language, who was at once foremost in criticism, supreme in fiction, and in poetry destined to be immortal.

From *Edgar Allan Poe: A Critical Biography* (New York: Appleton-Century, 1941), pp. 694-95.

VAN WYCK BROOKS: 1944

"A Seeker of the Perfect"

SICK OR WELL, he possessed, meanwhile, a literary genius that had had no parallel as yet on the American scene. This genius, moreover, was supremely artistic, as Cooper's, for instance, never was, or even the talent of Bryant, a lover of perfection; for Poe was a craftsman of exquisite skill in prose and verse alike, a conscious master of his methods as well as his effects. Even as a reviewer of books, he affirmed that reviews should be works of art, a point that no writer had thought of in America before, and Hawthorne alone was to rival him in the eighteen-thirties in the art of prose composition and the writing of tales. Irving, of course, was a natural artist, but he had little of the cunning of Poe, while Cooper, a man of genius, was nothing as a craftsman, and Poe was an innovator in verse, a creator of "novel forms of beauty," who influenced poets elsewhere for an age to come. A lover, as he said, of severe precision, profoundly excited by music,"[1] a seeker of the perfect who constantly revised his work, while disdaining all recourse to "poetic licence,"[2] he had taken to heart the remark of Bacon that "there is no excellent beauty that hath not some strangeness in the proportion." He had developed variations from the usual metrical patterns, notes that were subtly discordant and wholly unexpected, and, feeling that "the indefinite is an element of the true poesis," he sought "the unknown—the vague—the uncomprehended." His images, instead of creating specific pictures in the mind, evoked a world of sorrowful associations, remote, dim, sinister, melancholy, majestic, his refrains suggested echoes from bottomless gulfs, and when he repeated a word in a rhyme the sound seemed magically altered by the new collocation. One heard in a few of these brief poems a kind of ethereal music like Tennyson's horns of Elfland faintly blowing, though the dream-world of Poe was a wild weird clime indeed. It was haunted by ill angels, vast and formless, "flapping" from their condor wings invisible woe.

From *The World of Washington Irving* (New York: Dutton, 1944), pp. 364-65.

1. "I am profoundly excited by music and some poems—those of Tennyson especially—whom, with Keats, Shelley, Coleridge (occasionally), and a few others of like thought and expression, I regard as the *sole* poets."—Letter to Lowell.
2. "The true artist will avail himself of no 'licence' whatever."—*Marginalia.*

HOWARD MUMFORD JONES: 1944

Poe: Man of His Times

NOW POE was not, as Parrington seemed to think, merely an "aesthete and a craftsman" who "made a stir in the world." He was not merely a disappointed artist or merely a disgruntled and deracinated Southerner. He was, so to speak, a complete product of the publishing world of his time and of American taste and sensibility in the same epoch. The seventy-odd stories he wrote had been anticipated in almost all their aspects by British and American magazine fiction; and what Poe was principally trying to do was, like O. Henry and Ring Lardner, to master a market. His originality consisted in doing better than anybody else what everybody else was trying to do. His famous critical theories are to a surprising degree the rationale of successful magazine writing in his day. He had, to be sure, a difficult personality, but to think of Poe in terms of a damaged and therefore ineffectual angel, a misunderstood genius, a Satanic being, a problem for the psychologist and the belletrist only, is to give up literary history as an instrument for cultural analysis.

From *Ideas in America* (Cambridge: Harvard Univ. Press, 1944), p. 41.

T. S. ELIOT: 1949

A Want of "Maturity of Intellect"

POE IS indeed a stumbling block for the judicial critic. If we examine his work in detail, we seem to find in it nothing but slipshod writing, puerile thinking unsupported by wide reading or profound scholarship, haphazard experiments in various types of writing, chiefly under pressure of financial need, without perfection in any detail. This would not be just. But if, instead of regarding his work analytically, we take a distant view of it as a whole, we see a mass of unique shape and impressive size to which the eye constantly returns. . . .

He wrote very few poems, and of those few only half a dozen have had a great success: but those few are as well known to as large a number of people, are as well remembered by everybody, as any poems ever written. And some of his tales have had an important influence upon authors, and in types of writing where such influence would hardly be expected. . . .

It does not seem to me unfair to say that Poe has been regarded as a minor, or secondary, follower of the Romantic Movement: a successor to the so-called "Gothic" novelists in his fiction, and a follower of Byron and Shelley in his verse. This however is to place him in the English tradition; and there certainly he does not belong. English readers sometimes account for that in Poe which is outside of any English tradition, by saying that it is American; but this does not seem to me wholly true either, especially when we consider the other American writers of his own and an earlier generation. There is a certain flavour of provinciality about his work, in a sense in which Whitman is not in the least provincial: it is the provinciality of the person who is not at home where he belongs, but cannot get to anywhere else. Poe is a kind of displaced European; he is attracted to Paris, to Italy and to Spain, to places which he could endow with romantic gloom and grandeur. Although his ambit of movement hardly extended beyond the limits of Richmond and Boston longitudinally, and neither east nor west of these centres, he seems a wanderer with no fixed abode. There can be few authors of such eminence who have drawn so little from their own roots, who have been so isolated from any surroundings. . . .

That Poe had a powerful intellect is undeniable: but it seems to me the intellect of a highly gifted young person before puberty. The forms which his lively curiosity takes are those in which a pre-adolescent mentality delights: wonders of nature and of mechanics and of the supernatural, cryptograms and cyphers, puzzles and labyrinths, mechanical chess-players and wild flights of speculation. The variety and ardour of his curiosity delight and dazzle; yet in the end the eccentricity and lack of coherence of his interests tire. There is just that lacking which gives dignity to the mature man: a consistent view of life. An attitude can be mature and consistent, and yet be highly sceptical: but Poe was no sceptic. He appears to yield himself completely to the idea of the moment: the effect is, that all of his ideas seem to be *entertained* rather than believed. What is lacking is not brain power, but that maturity of intellect which comes only with the maturing of the man as a whole, the development and coordination of his various emotions. I am not concerned with any possible psychological or pathological explanation: it is enough for my purpose to record that the work of Poe is such as I should expect of a man of very exceptional mind and sensibility, whose emotional development has been in some respect arrested at an early age.

From "From Poe to Valéry," *The Hudson Review,* 2 (1949), 327, 329, 335; reprinted separately (New York: Harcourt, Brace, 1948).

ALLEN TATE: 1949

Our Obligation to Poe

IT WOULD be difficult for me to take Poe up, "study" him, and proceed to a critical judgment. One may give these affairs the look of method, and thus deceive almost everybody but oneself. In reading Poe we are not brought up against a large, articulate scheme of experience, such as we see adumbrated in Hawthorne or Melville, which we may partly sever from personal association, both in the writer and in ourselves. Poe surrounds us with Eliot's "wilderness of mirrors," in which we see a subliminal self endlessly repeated or, turning, a new posture of the same figure. It is not too harsh, I think, to say that it is stupid to suppose that by "evaluating" this forlorn demon in the glass, we dispose of him. For Americans, perhaps for most modern men, he is with us like a dejected cousin: we may "place" him but we may not exclude him from our board. This is the recognition of a relationship, almost of the blood, which we must in honor acknowledge: what destroyed him is potentially destructive of us. Not only this; we must acknowledge another obligation, if, like most men of my generation, we were brought up in houses where the works of Poe took their easy place on the shelf with the family Shakespeare and the early novels of Ellen Glasgow. This is the obligation of loyalty to one's experience: he was in our lives and we cannot pretend that he was not. Not even Poe's great power in Europe is quite so indicative of his peculiar "place" as his unquestioned, if unexamined, acceptance among ordinary gentle people whose literary culture was not highly developed. . . .

Poe's prose style, as well as certain qualities of his verse, expresses the kind of "reality" to which he had access: I believe I have indicated that it is a reality sufficiently terrible. In spite of an early classical education and a Christian upbringing, he wrote as if the experience of these traditions had been lost: he was well ahead of his time. He could not relate his special reality to a wider context of insights—a discipline that might have disciplined his prose. From the literary point of view he combined the primitive and the decadent: primitive, because he had neither history nor the historical sense; decadent, because he was the conscious artist of an intensity which lacked moral perspective. . . .

It may have been a condition of Poe's genius that his ignorance should have been what it was. If we read him as formal critics we shall be ready to see that it was another condition of his genius that he should never produce a poem or a story without blemishes, or a critical essay that, despite its acuteness in detail, does not evince provincialism of judgment and lack of knowledge. We must bear in mind Mr. Eliot's remark that Poe must be viewed as a whole. Even the fiction and the literary journalism that seem without value add to his massive impact upon the reader. . . .

From "Our Cousin, Mr. Poe." *The Forlorn Demon: Didactic and Critical Essays* (Chicago: Regnery, 1953), pp. 81-82, 93-94.

N. B. FAGIN: 1952

Poe's Literary Genius

FOR OUR DAY, it is best to forget the "tragedy" and the "mystery" of Poe and to make an end to the speculations—by preachers, social workers, and psychoanalysts—on what this son of obscure strolling players might have been had his adoption been legalized by Mr. Allan, had he not been a dipsomaniac, or had he married, not his little cousin Virginia but his "first" love, Elmira Royster, or some literary lady such as the ether-inhaling poetess Helen Whitman. Very likely he still would have written poetry—at eighteen he wrote to John Neal, a Yankee editor: "I . . . *am* a poet"—and very likely his poetry might have been of a somewhat different nature. But we write, and always have or should have, written about him essentially for the same reason that we read him, because he was the kind of literary artist that he was.

Poe practiced his craft as poet, critic, and story teller with diligence and dignity. His mother, he once boasted, had not hesitated to dedicate "her brief career of genius and beauty" to the stage; similarly, he never hesitated to dedicate his own brief career to literature. It was out of the question for him to follow in the footsteps of his parents: contempt for actors, which he had imbibed in the social milieu of the Allans of Richmond, prevented that. But he saw clearly that there would be no loss of dignity if he acted on the wider stage of the world at large as a "literary histrio." And this was what he did; he chose for himself the richly romantic part of a literary genius, supremely gifted, supremely contemptuous of the shallow demands of the world, supremely sensitive to beauty, original, imaginative, eccentric, a little mad perhaps, and Byronically self-assured, withdrawn, aloof.

He succeeded so well that to this day many serious critics refuse to accept him for what he was and for what he had so abundantly to give us and keep on wishing that he had been someone else and had written another kind of literature. In this respect, Poe's case is not unique, of course. Many winds of critical doctrine have blown over every major nineteenth-century American writer, but over none have they raged so vehemently and so pointlessly. Whenever criticism has believed that art needs no other justification than its own quality, Poe has been discovered to have sung wildly well. Whenever literature has been thought to be a criticism of life, a sociological or political weapon, or a means of transmitting moral precepts, he has been discovered to have been a minor and inconsequential writer. Yet through all these intellectual shifts his work has been read and continues to be read; certainly his poems and stories have had a steady circulation, and new editions of them have multiplied significantly.

From "Edgar Allan Poe," *The South Atlantic Quarterly,* 51 (1952), 279-80.

EDWARD H. DAVIDSON: 1957

Poe's Failings and Greatness

DESPITE THE EXCELLENCE of analytical and investigative research which has been directed into the life and works of Edgar Poe, the reputation of Poe, except at the popular level of adolescent reading confined to secondary education, is today quite low. His poetry is regarded as not very complex nor artful rimes by a poet who took the subject of poetry more seriously than his poetry demands. His short stories have their admirers, but the number of tales which still seem great are, at most, a mere half dozen; and his criticism, however much excitement it has always aroused in France, is considered to be based on a totally false methodology in terms of contemporary critical theory: Poe made the egregious mistake either of taking critical concepts into the "psychology" of the writer himself or of considering that a work of art is not only an autonomous but a unique creation which, as it were, is like the universe: it must be discovered as though nothing like it had ever appeared before. . . .

Poe's greatness lies in his few explorations into the dark underside of human consciousness, and subconsciousness—that variable world of thought, dream, and terror beyond life and knowledge. Poe best limned this world in incompleteness, in the gray dimension of our never knowing why the student in "The Raven" or Roderick Usher were driven mad or why the Man of the Crowd was obsessed to wander the streets of a modern city. Poe's art was the spectrum of symbolic irresolution; but then who could be final and complete in dealing with the mind's dark terror world of which it is itself unaware? His weakness was that he seldom thrust this drama of the haunted mind into the commonplace world where, as in Hawthorne's "Young Goodman Brown" or "Wakefield," the greatest terror exists. Poe's greatness lay in his projection of that horror in wholly new terms; he charted the way for farther, deeper ranges of symbolic extension. That "way" and the range of artistic perception will always be farther than any interpretive speculation can reach: with writers like Melville and Poe, there is no end to what the symbolic imagination can disclose.

From *Poe, A Critical Study* (Cambridge: The Belknap Press of Harvard Univ. Press, 1957), pp. 254, 260.

VINCENT BURANELLI: 1961

The Problem and Permanence of Poe

IF POE'S normal traits are being stressed too much today, it is an error on the right side, one that should enable us to strike a balance closer to the truth than either of the extremes. That he can ever be categorized neatly either biographically or artistically is not to be expected, for there is too much room for doubt and disputation when the ideas, moods and temperament of so difficult a personality are under investigation. But at least we are aware of the multifarious elements in him and his literature. . . .

He has the writer's greatest virtue of readability, for he writes prose that moves vigorously and is almost never dull; and he wields an art based on an economy of means—the ability to say in few words what another writer would say in many. He is a master of the great line. He writes with power, producing in his finest works the effect that follows from an understanding of what to say and how best to say it. He is original in that he invented one type of literature, perfected others, pointed out the way in which still others ought to be pursued. He is versatile: poet, storyteller, critic; artist in humor and horror and beauty and fantasy; genius of the Gothic tale, and of satire on the Gothic tale; romanticist, realist, symbolist, surrealist; author of "To Helen," "The Black Cat," "The Poetic Principle," "Eureka," and the review of Hawthorne.

From *Edgar Allan Poe* (New York: Twayne, 1961), pp. 19, 129.

EDWARD WAGENKNECHT: 1963

The Continuing Mystery

WE HAVE come a long way from the diabolical monster described by
Rufus Griswold who walked the streets murmuring curses under his
breath, accepting his own damnation as an established fact but interced-
ing, inconsistently, for those he loved. It is true that, as old errors die,
new errors are born, and that when we find new drugs to cure our
diseases, it may become necessary to devise fresh remedies to repair the
ravages of the drugs; though it quite lacks Griswold's viciousness, Marie
Bonaparte's interpretation of Poe is quite as fantastic as his. Nevertheless scholars have now disposed of a considerable quantity of nonsense
about Poe and established a considerable amount of positive fact.
Mystery there will always be about him, and perhaps it will always
require a certain kind of temperament to feel on easy terms with him,
but in this day and age anybody who considers him an atheist, a diabol-
ist, an immoralist, or a Gothic monster is simply unwilling to consider
the evidence at hand.

Few Americans have aspired more nobly than Poe, and, if he fell
short of his ideal, this should bring him closer to us and help us to
understand him better. His greatest fault was an instability which, despite all his capacity for work, made him unreliable in his personal
relationships, and he could be very trying when he donned a mask of
arrogance and bad manners to cover up this weakness. Whether his
faults were born with him or developed through the evil conditioning of
his life, it is not possible to say, for none of us has ever seen an
unconditioned man or handled unparticled matter. With all his faults,
however, and all the disadvantages he suffered, Poe did find those who
loved him while he was alive, and legions of readers have remained loyal
to him through the years, often in spite of the fact that they had no
means of discovering how good a man he really was.

From *Edgar Allan Poe: The Man Behind the Legend* (New York:
Oxford Univ. Press, 1963), pp. 220-21.

ROBERT D. JACOBS: 1969

Poe's "One Significant Accomplishment"

WE CAN credit him with one significant accomplishment. He described the purpose of the artist in terms which would make a purer art possible, and for this reason he has been more honored in France than in any country that follows the English tradition. He never became what Ortega y Gasset called the "pure nameless voice" of lyricism, but he entertained the possibility. Whether he be honored for it or condemned, Poe was the first critic in America to speak out boldly for the aesthetic purpose, even though he understood it imperfectly.

From *Poe: Journalist and Critic* (Baton Rouge: Louisiana State Univ. Press, 1969), p. 453.

General Critical Evaluations

JAMES W. GARGANO

The Question of Poe's Narrators

PART OF THE widespread critical condescension toward Edgar Allan Poe's short stories undoubtedly stems from impatience with what is taken to be his "cheap" or embarrassing Gothic style. Finding turgidity, hysteria, and crudely poetic overemphasis in Poe's works, many critics refuse to accept him as a really serious writer. Lowell's flashy indictment of Poe as "two-fifths sheer fudge"[1] agrees essentially with Henry James's magisterial declaration that an "enthusiasm for Poe is the mark of a decidedly primitive stage of reflection."[2] T. S. Eliot seems to be echoing James when he attributes to Poe "the intellect of a highly gifted young person before puberty."[3] Discovering in Poe one of the fountainheads of American obscurantism, Ivor Winters condemns the incoherence, puerility, and histrionics of his style. Moreover, Huxley's charge that Poe's poetry suffers from "vulgarity" of spirit, has colored the views of critics of Poe's prose style.[4]

Certainly, Poe has always had his defenders. One of the most brilliant of modern critics, Allen Tate finds a variety of styles in Poe's works; although Tate makes no high claims for Poe as stylist, he nevertheless points out that Poe could, and often did, write with lucidity and without Gothic mannerisms.[5] Floyd Stovall, a long-time and more enthusiastic admirer of Poe, has recently paid his critical respects to "the conscious art of Edgar Allan Poe."[6] Though he says little about Poe's style, he seems to me to suggest that the elements of Poe's stories, style for example, should be analyzed in terms of Poe's larger artistic intentions. Of course, other writers, notably Edward H. Davidson, have done much to demonstrate that an intelligible rationale informs Poe's best work.[7]

It goes without saying that Poe, like other creative men, is sometimes at the mercy of his own worst qualities. Yet the contention that he is fundamentally a bad or tawdry stylist appears to me to be rather facile and sophistical. It is based, ultimately, on the untenable and often unanalyzed assumption that Poe and his narrators are identical literary twins and that he must be held responsible for all their wild or perfervid utterances; their shrieks and groans are too often conceived as emanating from Poe himself. I believe, on the contrary, that Poe's narrators possess a character and consciousness distinct from those of their creator. These protagonists, I am convinced, speak their own

thoughts and are the dupes of their own passions. In short, Poe under-
stands them far better than they can possibly understand themselves.
Indeed, he often so designs his tales as to show his narrators' limited
comprehension of their own problems and states of mind; the structure
of many of Poe's stories clearly reveals an ironical and comprehensive
intelligence critically and artistically ordering events so as to establish a
vision of life and character which the narrator's very inadequacies help
to "prove."

What I am saying is simply that the total organization or completed
form of a work of art tells more about the author's sensibility than does
the report of confession of one of its characters. Only the most naive
reader, for example, will credit as the "whole truth" what the narrators
of *Barry Lyndon, Huckleberry Finn,* and *The Aspern Papers* will divulge about themselves and their experiences. In other words, the
"meaning" of a literary work (even when it has no narrator) is to be
found in its fully realized form; for only the entire work achieves the
resolution of the tensions, heterogeneities, and individual visions which
make up the parts. The Romantic apologists for Milton's Satan afford a
notorious example of the fallacy of interpreting a brilliantly integrated
poem from the point of view of its most brilliant character.

The structure of Poe's stories compels realization that they are more
than the effusions of their narrators' often disordered mentalities.
Through the irony of his characters' self-betrayal and through the development and arrangement of his dramatic actions, Poe suggests to his
readers ideas never entertained by the narrators. Poe intends his readers
to keep their powers of analysis and judgment ever alert; he does not
require or desire complete surrender to the experience of the sensations
being felt by his characters. The point of Poe's technique, then, is not
to enable us to lose ourselves in strange or outrageous emotions, but to
see these emotions and those obsessed by them from a rich and
thoughtful perspective. I do not mean to advocate that, while reading
Poe, we should cease to feel; but feeling should be "simultaneous" with
an analysis carried on with the composure and logic of Poe's great
detective, Dupin. For Poe is not merely a Romanticist; he is also a
chronicler of the consequences of the Romantic excesses which lead to
psychic disorder, pain, and disintegration.

Once Poe's narrative method is understood, the question of Poe's
style and serious artistry returns in a new guise. Clearly, there is often
an aesthetic compatibility between his narrators' hypertrophic language
and their psychic derangement; surely, the narrator in "Ligeia," whose
life is consumed in a blind rage against his human limitations, cannot be
expected to consider his dilemma in coolly rational prose. The language
of men reaching futilely towards the ineffable always runs the risk of
appearing more flatulent than inspired. Indeed, in the very breakdown
of their visions into lurid and purple rhetoric, Poe's characters enforce

the message of failure that permeates their aspirations and actions. The narrator in "Ligeia" blurts out, in attempting to explain his wife's beauty in terms of its "expression": "Ah, words of no meaning!" He rants about "incomprehensible anomalies," "words that are impotent to convey," and his inability to capture the "inexpressible." He raves because he cannot explain. His feverish futility of expression, however, cannot be attributed to Poe, who with an artistic "control," documents the stages of frustration and fantastic desire which end in the narrator's madness. The completed action of "Ligeia," then, comments on the narrator's career of self-delusion and exonerates Poe from the charge of lapsing into self-indulgent, sentimental rodomantade.

In "The Tell-Tale Heart" the cleavage between author and narrator is perfectly apparent. The sharp exclamations, nervous questions, and broken sentences almost too blatantly advertise Poe's conscious intention, the protagonists's painful insistence in "proving" himself sane only serves to intensify the idea of his madness. Once again Poe presides with precision of perception at the psychological drama he describes. He makes us understand that the voluble murderer has been tortured by the nightmarish terrors he attributes to his victim: "He was sitting up in bed listening;—just as I have done, night after night, harkening to the death watches in the wall"; further the narrator interprets the old man's groan in terms of his own persistent anguish: "Many a night, just at midnight, when all the world slept, it has welled up from my own bosom, deepening, with its dreadful echo, the terrors that distracted me." Thus, Poe, in allowing his narrator to disburden himself of his tale, skillfully contrives to show also that he lives in a haunted and eerie world of his own demented making.

Poe assuredly knows what the narrator never suspects and what, by the controlled conditions of the tale, he is not meant to suspect—that the narrator is a victim of his own self-torturing obsessions. Poe so manipulates the action that the murder, instead of freeing the narrator, is shown to heighten his agony and intensify his delusions. The watches in the wall become the ominously beating heart of the old man, and the narrator's vaunted self-control explodes into a frenzy that leads to self-betrayal. I find it almost impossible to believe that Poe has no serious artistic motive in "The Tell-Tale Heart," that he merely revels in horror and only inadvertently illuminates the depths of the human soul. I find it equally difficult to accept the view that Poe's style should be assailed because of the ejaculatory and crazy confession of his narrator.

For all of its strident passages, "William Wilson" once again exhibits in its well-defined structure a sense of authorial poise which contrasts markedly with the narrator's confusion and blindness. Wilson's story is organized in six parts: a rather "over-written" *apologia* for his life; a long account of his early student days at Dr. Bransby's grammar school, where he is initiated into evil and encounters the second Wilson; a brief section on his wild behavior at Eton; an episode showing his black-guardly conduct at Oxford; a non-dramatic description of his flight from his namesake-pursuer; and a final, climactic scene in which he confronts and kills his "double." The incidents are so arranged as to trace the "development" of Wilson's wickedness and moral blindness. Moreover, Poe's conscious artistic purpose is evident in the effective functioning of many details of symbolism and setting. "Bright rays" from a lamp enable Wilson to see his nemesis "vividly" at Dr. Bransby's; at the critical appearance of his double at Eton, Wilson's perception is obscured by a "faint light"; and in the scene dealing with Wilson's exposé at Oxford, the darkness becomes almost total and the intruder's presence is "felt" rather than seen. Surely, this gradual extinction of light serves to point up the darkening of the narrator's vision. The setting at Dr. Bransby's school, where it was impossible to determine "upon which of its two stories one happened to be," cleverly enforces Poe's theme of the split consciousness plaguing Wilson. So, too, does the portrait of the preacher-pastor: "This reverend man, with counten-ance so demurely benign, with robes so glossy and so clerically flowing, with wig so minutely powdered, so rigid and so vast,—could this be he who, of late, with sour visage and in snuffy habiliments, administered, ferule in hand, the Draconian laws of the academy? Oh, gigantic para-dox, too utterly monstrous for solution!" Finally, the masquerade setting in the closing scene of the tale ingeniously reveals that Wilson's whole life is a disguise from his own identity.

To maintain that Poe has stumbled into so much organization as can be discovered in "William Wilson" and his other tales requires the sup-port of strong prejudice. There seems little reason for resisting the conclusion that Poe knows what ails Wilson and sees through his narra-tor's lurid self-characterization as a "victim to the horror and the mystery of the wildest of all sublunary visions." Assuredly, a feeling for the design and subtlety of Poe's "William Wilson" should exorcise the idea that he is as immature and "desperate" as his protagonist. After all, Poe created the situations in which Wilson confronts and is confronted by his *alter ego;* it is Wilson who refuses to meet, welcome, and be restrained by him.

Evidence of Poe's "seriousness" seems to me indisputable in "The Cask of Amontillado," a tale which W. H. Auden has belittled.[8] Far from being his author's mouthpiece, the narrator, Montresor, is one of the supreme examples in fiction of a deluded rationalist who cannot glimpse the moral implications of his planned folly. Poe's fine ironic sense makes clear that Montresor, the stalker of Fortunato, is both a compulsive and pursued man; for in committing a flawless crime against another human being, he really (like Wilson and the protagonist in "The Tell-Tale Heart") commits the worst of crimes against himself. His reasoned, "cool" intelligence weaves an intricate plot which, while

ostensibly satisfying his revenge, despoils him of humanity. His impec-
cably contrived murder, his weird mask of goodness in an enterprise of
evil, and his abandonment of all his life-energies in one pet project of
hate convict him of a madness which he mistakes for the inspiration of
genius. The brilliant masquerade setting of Poe's tale intensifies the
theme of Montresor's apparently successful duplicity; Montresor's
ironic appreciation of his own deviousness seems further to justify his
arrogance of intellect. But the greatest irony of all, to which Montresor
is never sensitive, is that the "injuries" supposedly perpetrated by Fortunato are illusory and that the vengeance meant for the victim recoils
upon Montresor himself. In immolating Fortunato, the narrator unconsciously calls him the "noble" Fortunato and confesses that his own
"heart grew sick." Though Montresor attributes this sickness to "the
dampness of the catacombs," it is clear that his crime has begun to
"possess" him. We see that, after fifty years, it remains the obsession of
his life; the meaning of his existence resides in the tomb in which he
has, symbolically, buried himself. In other words, Poe leaves little
doubt that the narrator has violated his own mind and humanity, that
the external act has had its destructive inner consequences.

The same artistic integrity and seriousness of purpose evident in
"The Cask of Amontillado" can be discovered in "The Black Cat." No
matter what covert meanings one may find in this much-discussed
story, it can hardly be denied that the nameless narrator does not speak
for Poe. Whereas the narrator, at the beginning of his "confession,"
admits that he cannot explain the events which overwhelmed him, Poe's
organization of his episodes provides an unmistakable clue to his protagonist's psychic deterioration. The tale has two distinct, almost parallel parts: in the first, the narrator's inner moral collapse is presented
in largely symbolic narrative; in the second part, the consequences of
his self-violation precipitate an act of murder, punishable by society.
Each section of the story deals with an ominous cat, an atrocity, and an
exposé of a "crime." In the first section, the narrator's house is consumed by fire after he has mutilated and subsequently hanged Pluto, his
pet cat. Blindly, he refuses to grant any connection between his violence and the fire; yet the image of a hanged cat on the one remaining
wall indicates that he will be haunted and hag-ridden by his deed. The
sinister figure of Pluto, seen by a crowd of neighbors, is symbolically
both an accusation and a portent, an enigma to the spectators but an
infallible sign to the reader.

In the second section of "The Black Cat," the reincarnated cat goads
the narrator into the murder of his wife. As in "William Wilson," "The
Tell-Tale Heart," and "The Cask of Amontillado," the narrator cannot
understand that his assault upon another person derives from his own
moral sickness and unbalance. Like his confreres, too, he seeks psychic
release and freedom in a crime which completes his torture. To the end

of his life, he is incapable of locating the origin of his evil and damnation within himself.

The theme of "The Black Cat" is complicated for many critics by the narrator's dogged assertion that he was pushed into evil and self-betrayal by the "imp of the perverse." This imp is explained, by a man who, it must be remembered, eschews explanation, as a radical, motiveless, and irresistible impulse within the human soul. Consequently, if his self-analysis is accepted, his responsibility for his evil life vanishes. Yet, it must be asked if it is necessary to give credence to the words of the narrator. William Wilson, too, regarded himself as a "victim" of a force outside himself and Montresor speaks as if he has been coerced into his crime by Fortunato. The narrator in "The Black Cat" differs from Wilson in bringing to his defense a well-reasoned theory with perhaps a strong appeal to many readers. Still, the narrator's pat explanation is contradicted by the development of the tale, for instead of being pushed into crime, he pursues a life which makes crime inevitable. He cherishes the intemperate self-indulgence which blunts his powers of self-analysis; he is guided by his delusions to the climax of damnation. Clearly, Poe does not espouse his protagonist's theory any more than he approves of the specious rationalizations of his other narrators. Just as the narrator's well constructed house has a fatal flaw, so the theory of perverseness is flawed because it really explains nothing. Moreover, even the most cursory reader must be struck by the fact that the narrator is most "possessed and maddened" when he most proudly boasts of his self-control. If the narrator obviously cannot be believed at the end of the tale, what argument is there for assuming that he must be telling the truth when he earlier tries to evade responsibility for his "sin" by slippery rationalizations?

A close analysis of "The Black Cat" must certainly exonerate Poe of the charge of merely sensational writing. The final frenzy of the narrator, with its accumulation of superlatives, cannot be ridiculed as an example of Poe's style. The breakdown of the shrieking criminal does not reflect a similar breakdown in the author. Poe, I maintain, is a serious artist who explores the neuroses of his characters with probing intelligence. He permits his narrator to revel and flounder into torment, but he sees beyond the torment to its causes.

In conclusion, then, the five tales I have commented on display Poe's deliberate craftsmanship and penetrating sense of irony. If my thesis is correct, Poe's narrators should not be construed as his mouthpieces; instead they should be regarded as expressing, in "charged" language indicative of their internal disturbances, their own peculiarly nightmarish visions. Poe, I contend, is conscious of the abnormalities of his narrators and does not condone the intellectual ruses through which they strive, only too earnestly, to justify themselves. In short, though his narrators are often febrile or demented, Poe is conspicuously "sane." They may be "decidedly primitive" or "wildly incoherent," but Poe, in his stories at least, is mature and lucid.

From *College English,* 25 (1963), 177-81.

1. "A Fable for Critics," *The Complete Poetical Works of James Russell Lowell* (Cambridge, 1896), p. 140.

2. Henry James, "Charles Baudelaire," *French Poets and Novelists* (London, 1878).

3. T. S. Eliot, "From Poe to Valéry," p. 28.

4. Aldous Huxley, "Vulgarity in Literature," *Music at Night and Other Essays* (London, 1949), pp. 297-309.

5. Allen Tate, "Our Cousin, Mr. Poe," *The Man of Letters in the Modern World,* Meridian Books, pp. 132-145.

6. Floyd Stovall, "The Conscious Art of Edgar Allan Poe," *College English,* 24 (March 1963), 417-421.

7. Davidson, *Poe: A Critical Study* (Cambridge, 1957).

8. Auden, "Introduction" to *Edgar Allan Poe: Selected Prose and Poetry,* Rinehart Editions, p.v.

BRANDER MATTHEWS

Poe and the Detective Story

THE DETECTIVE STORY which Poe invented sharply differentiates itself from the earlier tales of mystery, and also from the later narratives in which actual detectives figure incidentally. Perhaps the first of these tales of mystery is Walpole's "Castle of Otranto," which appears to us now clumsy enough, with its puerile attempts to excite terror. The romances of Mrs. Radcliffe are scarcely more solidly built—indeed, the fatigue of the sophisticated reader of to-day when he undertakes the perusal of these old-fashioned and long-winded chronicles may be ascribed partly to the flimsiness of the foundation which is supposed to support the awe-inspiring superstructure. Godwin's "Caleb Williams" is far more firmly put together; and its artful planning called for imagination as well as mere invention. In the "Edgar Huntley" of Charles Brockden Brown the veil of doubt skilfully shrouds the unsuspected and unsuspecting murderer who did the evil deed in his sleep—anticipating the somnambulist hero of Wilkie Collins's "Moonstone.". . .

In the true detective story as Poe conceived it in the "Murders in the Rue Morgue," it is not in the mystery itself that the author seeks to interest the reader, but rather in the successive steps whereby his analytic observer is enabled to solve a problem that might well be dismissed as beyond human elucidation. Attention is centred on the unravelling of the tangled skein rather than on the knot itself. The emotion aroused is not mere surprise, it is recognition of the unsuspected capabilities of the human brain; it is not a wondering curiosity as to an airless mechanism, but a heightening admiration for the analytic acumen capable of working out an acceptable answer to the puzzle propounded. In other words, Poe, while he availed himself of the obvious advantages of keeping a secret from his readers and of leaving them guessing as long as he pleased, shifted the point of attack and succeeded in giving a human interest to his tale of wonder.

And by this shift Poe transported the detective story from the group of tales of adventure into the group of portrayals of character. By bestowing upon it a human interest, he raised it in the literary scale. There is no need now to exaggerate the merits of this feat or to suggest that Poe himself was not capable of loftier efforts. Of course the "Fall of the House of Usher," which is of imagination all compact, is more valid evidence of his genius than the "Murders in the Rue Morgue," which is the product rather of his invention, supremely ingenious as it is. Even though the detective story as Poe produced it is elevated far above the barren tale of mystery which preceded it and which has been revived in our own day, it is not one of the loftiest of literary forms, and its possibilities are severely limited. It suffers to-day from the fact that in the half century and more since Poe set the pattern it has been vulgarized, debased, degraded by a swarm of imitators who lacked his certainty of touch, his instinctive tact, his intellectual individuality. In their hands it has been bereft of its distinction and despoiled of its atmosphere.

Even at its best, in the simple perfection of form that Poe bestowed on it, there is no denying that it demanded from its creator no depth of sentiment, no warmth of emotion, and no large understanding of human desire. There are those who would dismiss it carelessly, as making an appeal not far removed from that of the riddle and of the conundrum. There are those again who would liken it rather to the adroit trick of a clever conjurer. No doubt, it gratifies in us chiefly that delight in difficulty conquered, which is a part of the primitive play impulse potent in us all, but tending to die out as we feel more deeply the tragi-comedy of existence. But inexpensive as it may seem to those of us who look to literature for enlightenment, for solace in the hour of need, for stimulus to stiffen the will in the never-ending struggle of life, the detective tale, as Poe contrived it, has merits of its own as distinct and as undeniable as those of the historical novel, for example, or of the sea tale. It may please the young rather than the old, but the pleasure it can give is ever innocent; and the young are always in the majority.

In so far as Poe had any predecessor in the composing of a narrative, the interest of which should reside in the application of human intelligence to the solution of a mystery, this was not Balzac, although the American romancer was sufficiently familiar with "Human Comedy" to venture an unidentified quotation from it. Nor was this predecessor Cooper, whom Balzac admired and even imitated, although Leatherstocking in tracking his redskin enemies revealed the tense observation and the faculty of deduction with which Poe was to endow his Dupin. The only predecessor with a good claim to be considered a progenitor is Voltaire, in whose "Zadig" we can find the method which Poe was to apply more elaborately. The Goncourts perceived this descent of Poe from Voltaire when they recorded in their "Journal" that the strange tales of the American poet seemed to them to belong to "a new literature, the literature of the twentieth century, scientifically miraculous story-telling by A + B, a literature at once monomaniac and mathematical, Zadig as district attorney, Cyrano de Bergerac as a pupil of Arago.". . .

Huxley has pointed out that the method of Zadig is the method which has made possible the incessant scientific discovery of the last century. It is the method of Wellington at Assaye, assuming that there must be a ford at a certain place on the river, because there was a village on each side. It is the method of Grant at Vicksburg, examining the knapsacks of the Confederate soldiers slain in a sortie to see if these contained rations, which would show that the garrison was seeking to break out because the place was untenable. It is also the method of Poe in the "Gold Bug" and in the "Murders in the Rue Morgue."

In his application of this method, not casually, playfully, and with satiric intent, as Voltaire had applied it, but seriously and taking it as the mainspring of his story, Poe added an ingenious improvement of his own devising. Upon the preternaturally acute observer who was to control the machinery of the tale, the American poet bestowed a companion of only an average alertness and keenness; and to this commonplace companion the romancer confided the telling of the story. By this seemingly simple device Poe doubled the effectiveness of his work, because this unobservant and unimaginative narrator of the unravelling of a tangled skein by an observant and imaginative analyst naturally recorded his own admiration and astonishment as the wonder was wrought before his eyes, so that the admiration and astonishment were transmitted directly and suggestively to the readers of the narrative.

In the "Gold Bug" the wonder worker is Legrand, and in both the "Murders in the Rue Morgue" and the "Purloined Letter" he is M. Dupin; and in all three tales the telling of the story is entrusted to an anonymous narrator, serving not only as a sort of Greek chorus to hint to the spectators the emotions they ought to feel, but also as the describer of the personality and peculiarities of Legrand and Dupin, who are thus individualized, humanized, and related to the real world. If they had not been accepted by the narrator as actual beings of flesh and blood, they might otherwise retain the thinness and the dryness of disembodied intelligences working in a vacuum.

This device of the transmitting narrator is indisputably valuable; and, properly enough, it reappears in the one series of detective tales which may be thought by some to rival Poe's. The alluring record of the investigations of Mr. Sherlock Holmes is the world of a certain Dr. Watson, a human being but little more clearly characterized than the anonymous narrators who have preserved for us the memory of Legrand and Dupin. But Poe here again exhibited a more artistic reserve than any of his imitators, in so far as he refrained from the undue laudation of the strange intellectual feats which are the central interest of these three tales. In the "Gold Bug" he even heightens his suspense by allowing the narrator to suggest that the Legrand might be of unsound mind: and in the "Murders in the Rue Morgue" the narrator, although lost in astonishment at the acuteness of Dupin, never permits his admiration to become fulsome; he holds himself in, as though fear-ing that overpraise might provoke a denial. Moreover, Poe refrained from all exhibitions of Dupin's skill merely for its own sake—exhibitions only dazzling the spectators and not furthering his immediate purpose.

Nothing could be franker than Sir Conan Doyle's acknowledgment of his indebtedness. "Edgar Allen [sic] Poe, who, in his carelessly prodi-gal fashion, threw out the seeds from which so many of our present forms of literature have sprung, was the father of the detective tale, and covered its limits so completely that I fail to see how his followers can find any fresh ground which they can confidently call their own. For the secret of the thinness and also of the intensity of the detective story is that the writer is left with only one quality, that of intellectual acuteness, with which to endow his hero. Everything else is outside the picture and weakens the effect. The problem and its solution must form the theme, and the character drawing is limited and subordinate. On this narrow path the writer must walk, and he sees the footmarks of Poe always in front of him. He is happy if he ever finds the means of breaking away and striking out on some little side-track of his own."

The deviser of the adventures of Sherlock Holmes hit on a happy phrase when he declared that "the problem and its solution must form the theme." This principle was violated by Dumas, who gave us the solution before the problem, when he showed how d'Artagnan used the method of Zadig to deduce all the details of the duel on horseback, in the "Vicomte de Bragelonne," after the author had himself described to us the incidents of that fight. But when he was thus discounting his effect Dumas probably had in mind, not Poe, but Cooper, whose obser-vant redskins he mightily admired and whom he frankly imitated in the "Mohicans of Paris."

Although Poe tells these three stories in the first person, as if he was himself only the recorder of the marvellous deeds of another, both Legrand and Dupin are projections of his own personality; they are characters created by him to be endowed with certain of his own quali-fications and peculiarities. They were called into being to be possessed of the inventive and analytical powers of Poe himself. "To be an artist, first and always, requires a turn for induction and analysis"—so Mr. Stedman has aptly put it; and this turn for induction and analysis Poe had far more obviously than most artists. When he was a student he excelled in mathematics; in all his other tales he displays the same power of logical construction; and he delighted in the exercise of his own acumen, vaunting his ability to translate any cipher that might be sent to him and succeeding in making good his boast. In the criticism of "Barnaby Rudge," and again in the explanation of the Maelzel chess-player, Poe used for himself the same faculty of divination, the same power of seizing the one clue needful, however tangled amid other threads, which he had bestowed upon Legrand and Dupin.

If we may exclude the "Marie Roger" narrative in which Poe was working over an actual case of murder, we find him only three times undertaking the "tale of ratiocination," to use his own term; and in all three stories he was singularly happy in the problem he invented for solution. For each of the three he found a fit theme, wholly different from that employed in either of the others. He adroitly adjusted the proper accessories, and he created an appropriate atmosphere. With no sense of strain, and no awkwardness of manner, he dealt with episodes strange indeed, but so simply treated as to seem natural, at least for the moment. There is no violence of intrigue or conjecture; indeed Poe strives to suggest a background of the commonplace against which his marvels may seem the more marvellous. In none of his stories is Poe's consummate mastery of the narrative art, his ultimate craftsmanship, his certain control of all the devices of the most accomplished story-teller, more evident than in these three.

And yet they are but detective stories, after all; and Poe himself, never prone to underestimate what he had written, spoke of them lightly and even hinted that they had been overpraised. Probably they were easy writing—for him—and therefore they were not so close to his heart as certain other of his tales over which he had toiled long and more laboriously. Probably also he felt the detective story to be an inferior form. However superior his stories in this kind might be, he knew them to be unworthy of comparison with his more imaginative tales, which he had filled with a thrilling weirdness and which attained a soaring elevation far above any height to be achieved by ingenious narratives setting forth the solving of a puzzle.

It is in a letter to Philip Pendleton Cooke, written in 1846, that Poe disparaged his detective stories and declared that they "owe most of their popularity to being something in a new key. I do not mean to say that they are not ingenious—but people think them more ingenious than they are—on account of their method and *air* of method. In the 'Murders in the Rue Morgue,' for instance, where is the ingenuity of unravelling a web which you yourself (the author) have woven for the express pur-pose of unravelling? The reader is made to confound the ingenuity of the supposititious Dupin with that of the writer of the story." Here, surely, Poe is overmodest; at least he overstates the case against himself. The ingenuity of the author obviously lies in his invention of a web which seemingly cannot be unravelled and which nevertheless one of the characters of the tale, Legrand or Dupin, succeeds in unravelling at last. This ingenuity may be, in one way, less than that required to solve an actual problem in real life; but it is also, in another way, more, for it had to invent its own puzzle and to put this together so that the secret seemed to be absolutely hidden, although all the facts needed to solve it were plainly presented to the reader.

In the same letter to Cooke, Poe remarked on the "wide diversity and variety" of his tales when contrasted one with another; and he asserted that he did not consider any one better than another. "There is a vast variety of kinds, and in degree of value these kinds vary—but each tale is equally good *of its kind.*" He added that "the loftiest kind is that of the highest imagination." For this reason only he considered that "Ligeia" might be called the best of his stories. Now, after a lapse of threescore years, the "Fall of the House of Usher," with its "serene and sombre beauty," would seem to deserve the first place of all. And among the detective stories, standing on a lower plane as they do, because they were wrought by invention rather than by the interpreting imagination, the foremost position may be given to the "Murders in the Rue Morgue." In this tale Poe's invention is most ingenious and his subject is selected with the fullest understanding of the utmost possibilities of the detective story. At the core of it is a strange, mysterious, monstrous crime; and M. Anatole France was never wiser than when he declared the unfailing interest of mankind in a gigantic misdeed "because we find in all crimes that fund of hunger and desire on which we all live, the good as well as the bad." Before a crime such as this we seem to find ourselves peering into the contorted visage of primitive man, obeying no law but his own caprice.

The superiority of the poet who wrote the first detective story over all those who have striven to tread in the trail he blazed is obvious enough. It resides not only in his finer workmanship, his more delicate art, his finer certainty of execution, his more absolute knowledge of what it was best to do and of the way best to do this; it is to be seen not only in his command of verisimilitude, in his plausibility, in his faculty of enwrapping the figures of his narrative in the atmosphere most fit for them; it is not in any of these things or in all of them that Poe's supremacy is founded. The reason of that supremacy must be sought in the fact that, after all, Poe was of a truth a poet, and that he had the informing imagination of a poet, even though it was only the more prosaic side of the faculty divine which he chose to employ in these tales of ratiocination.

It is by their possession of poetry, however slight their portion might be, that Fitzjames O'Brien and M. Jean Richepin and Mr. Rudyard Kipling were kept from rank failure when they followed in Poe's footsteps and sought to imitate, or at least to emulate his more largely imaginative tales in the "Diamond Lens" of the Irish-American, in the "Morts Bizarres" of the Frenchman, and in half a dozen tales of the Anglo-Indian. But what tincture of poesy, what sweep of vision, what magic of style, is there in the attempts of the most of the others who have taken pattern by his detective stories? None, and less than none. Ingenuity of a kind there is in Gaboriau's longer fictions, and in those of Fortuné de Boisgobey, and in those of Wilkie Collins; but this ingenuity is never so simply employed, and it is often artificial and violent and mechanical. It exists for its own sake, with little relation to the admitted characteristics of our common humanity. It stands alone, and it is never accompanied by the apparent ease which adds charm to Poe's handling of his puzzles.

Consider how often Gaboriau puts us off with a broken-backed narrative, taking up his curtain on a promising problem, presenting it to us in aspects of increasing difficulty, only at last to confess his impotence by starting afresh and slowly detailing the explanatory episodes which happened before the curtain rose. Consider how frequently Fortuné de Boisgobey failed to play fair. Consider how juiceless was the documentary method of Wilkie Collins, how mechanical and how arid, how futilely complicated, how prolonged, and how fatiguing. Consider all the minor members of the sorry brood hatched out of the same egg, how cheap and how childish the most of them are. Consider all these; and we are forced to the conclusion that if the writing of a good detective story is so rare and so difficult, if only one of Poe's imitators has been able really to rival his achievement, if this single success has been the result of an acceptance of Poe's formula and of a close adherence to Poe's practice, then, what Poe wrought is really unique; and we must give him the guerdon of praise due to an artist who has accomplished the first time of trying that which others have failed to achieve even after he had shown them how.

From "Poe and the Detective Story," *Scribner's Magazine*, 42 (1907), 287-93.

CONSTANCE ROURKE

Humor in Poe

OF ALL American writers Poe has become a symbol for the type of genius which rises clear from its time, nourished mainly from hidden inner sources. Poe himself would have delighted in that theory, for he fostered the conviction that he ranged over only the rarest and most esoteric materials. But Poe came from the Scotch-Irish stock with its heritage of unsettlement from which were drawn the scouts and myth-makers and many strollers of the West; the theatrical strain that had been strong among them was his by birth; and he began to write at the end of the '20's when American myth-making was passing into its great popular diffusion. Essential foreign influences on Poe have been discovered, but in general the influences which weigh most with any writer are those which are akin to his own feeling and purposes. Poe drew upon German and French romanticism: but a homely romantic movement of native origin was making itself felt nearer at hand; and Poe both by temperament and environment was susceptible to the native forces.

The impact of popular comic story-telling in America must have reached Poe. At his foster-father's house Negro legends were surely current among the slaves; he must have heard the exploits of those adventurers by land and sea who drifted into the office of Allan and Company. Since this firm were agents for subscriptions to newspapers Poe no doubt had access to the current almanacs, which even in an early day were beginning to print compact stories of wild adventure. He may have seen tales of buccaneering and of buried treasure there, preparing him for *The Gold Bug,* or of hazards at sea, which suggested *Arthur Gordon Pym.* At the University of Virginia a few of his companions were accomplished in the western art of biting and gouging; probably story-telling was exhibited as another form of prowess. Poe himself gained a reputation as an amusing story-teller in these years. At Baltimore in 1831 and 1832 he could hardly have missed echoes of western story-telling, for Baltimore was a point of convergence for travelers from all that wide circle known as the Southwest; they came on horseback or by stage over the mountains, by boat from Savannah or New Orleans. Their appearance was striking: their talk and tales were caught fragmentarily by many observers. At the theaters the backwoodsman was being portrayed in the semblance of Crockett; and the new stage character was creating a highly novel sensation.

That broad grotesque myth-making which had to do with corn-crackers and country rapscallions Poe surely encountered, for in 1835 he reviewed Longstreet's *Georgia Scenes,* with enthusiasm. When Poe went to Philadelphia, always a center for the comic theater, the larger pattern of native figures must again have moved before him, and surely his association with Burton on the *Gentleman's Magazine* gave an impetus to his sense of native comedy, for though Burton's alliance with Brougham lay in the future, he had long been a comedian and had compiled comic joke-books and song-books. Poe possessed besides what Woodberry has called "a contemporaneous mind." He quickly turned to matters of current interest, exploration, treasure-hunting, mesmerism, Masonry, balloons, topics that crowded the newspapers and were being discussed by popular lecturers. He turned to comedy; as by instinct he turned to the hoax. His early *Journal of Julius Rodman* purported to give a literal account of a western journey and was essentially a hoax, as was his *Arthur Gordon Pym* with its studied effort to produce an effect of truth. His *Hans Pfall* was in the vanguard of a long sequence of hoaxes, anticipating by only a brief space Locke's famous Moon Hoax, which made a great stir in 1835. With its carefully prepared verisimilitude even to effects of costuming, with its intense stress of all outward sensation, *Hans Pfall* bore a close resemblance to the more elaborate and finished tall tales of the West, which were scrupulous as to detail and which often gave—as it happened—a particularly keen attention to costume. His *Balloon Hoax* in 1844 had its brief day of acceptance as fact. One of Poe's last stories, *Von Kempelen and His Discovery,* was essentially a hoax; and his talent for comic fantasy was shown in still another form in a topsy-turvy extravaganza, *The Angel of the Odd.*

Poe never used native legends directly except perhaps in *The Gold Bug;* yet in creative bent he was perhaps one of those major writers who instinctively turn toward long-established traditions. Unrooted in any region—if indeed any American of those years could be called rooted—he found no long and substantial accumulation of native materials, even though the comic myth-making faculty was abroad in force during his later youth. None the less Poe followed a course habitually followed by traditional writers and myth-makers: he did not invent, he borrowed and re-created. His *King Pest* was built upon a scene from *Vivian Gray;* he borrowed indeed at every turn.

Even if native legends had been strewn about with unmistakable richness one cannot be sure that Poe would have used them. That restless impulse which had driven other story-tellers farther and farther afield might have moved him. But the patterns, if not the substance of his tales, were those of a native story-telling. The gamut of his moods might have been drawn from the West, plumbing horror, yet turning also to a wild contrived comedy. Because of his own dark fate, and because Poe himself often stressed the *frisson,* terror has overtopped comedy in the general apprehension of his tales. His designations of "grotesque" and "arabesque" and his later "tales of terror" have created a further submergence of the comic. Yet *King Pest,* with its background of the plague and the night, is one of the most brilliant pure burlesques in the language, transmuting terror into gross comedy, as it had often been transmuted in the western tall tales.

According to Poe's original plan for the *Tales of the Folio Club* each member of the Club was to be satirically described; after the telling of each tale they were to criticize it, their comments forming a burlesque of criticism. The tales run through a wide range of humor, from the sheer absurdity of *Lionising* to the hoax of *Hans Pfall.* The Duc in *The Duc de l'Omelette* bore some relation to those derisive portraits of foreigners which were steadily gaining American favor; he was even given a not inharmonious touch of diabolism. Poe's command of verbal humor was uncertain; his puns often fall below tolerable levels. Yet these too are part of the mode of the time—a time when language was being carelessly and comically turned upside down and even re-created, as if to form a new and native idiom.

His laughter was of a single order: it was inhuman, and mixed with hysteria. His purpose in the hoaxes was to make his readers absurd, to reduce them to an involuntary imbecility. His objective was triumph, the familiar objective of popular comedy. To this end, in his burlesques and extravaganzas, he showed human traits or lineaments in unbelievable distortion, using that grotesquerie which lies midway between the comic and the terrible; with Poe the terrible was always within view. There are touches of chilly barbarity even in *Hans Pfall.* The fantasy-making of the West had swung from an impinging terror to a gross and often brutal comedy; Poe also stressed black moods and emotions, embracing a dark and ghostly melodrama, employing themes bordering upon those in the romantic tragedy of the day. In the midst of burlesque in *Tales of the Folio Club* he reached an antithetical horror, in *Berenice.*

Western story-telling had often been callous: in callousness Poe could pass beyond human limits, in the *Facts in the Case of M. Valdemar.* He used the magnified scale in rooms, corridors, draperies, in the accumulation of detail, in sensation. He enjoyed mystification; his tone and level throughout were those of legend; and if his scope in storytelling was brief he verged toward larger forms. His *Tales of the Folio Club* were made to follow in a prismatic sequence, and other stories fall into loosely united cycles.

Poe entered another area marked out by the popular comic tradition: that of the inner mind or consciousness. Not only Emerson approached this, or Thoreau in the delicate exemplification of inner states, or Whitman in his outpourings. Poe—and also Hawthorne, and even Melville—invaded this area and in some measure conquered it. Poe used the first person continually, adopting it in part perhaps to gain an impulse toward an exploration of states of mind or feeling which were often undoubtedly his own. Beyond direct transcriptions, which may have been unconscious, he clearly attempted to explore the character of the inner, even the sub-conscious, mind. In *The Black Cat* he dwelt on "the spirit of PERVERSENESS. . . . Yet I am not more sure that my soul lives than I am that perverseness is one of the primitive impulses of the human heart—one of the indivisible primary faculties or sentiments which give direction to the character of Man. . . . " He mentioned the "unfathomable longing of the soul *to vex itself*—to offer violence to its own nature." He made notations on small crises of the mind, speaking in *Ligeia* of the endeavor to recall to memory something forgotten when "we often find ourselves upon *the very verge* of remembrance, without being able in the end to remember." These fragmentary touches and others like them scattered through Poe's tales culminated in his story of double identity in *William Wilson,* in which memory—its obscure envelopments, its buried treasures—made a recurrent theme. Half symbolical, half factual, filled by intimations of a complex and warring inner state. *William Wilson* stands as a fresh creation in an almost untouched field, a prelude to the so-called psychological novel, and a further revelation of a native bias.

In critical theory the psychological strain has sometimes been linked with the Puritan influences; but surely no tie with the Puritan faith and its habit of introspection can be found for Poe. By birth and upbringing and sympathy he was wholly alien to the Puritan strain. Nothing remotely moralistic can be found in his observation, no identity with religious feeling, no judgments. Instead, Poe seems near those story-tellers of the West who described wild and perverse actions with blank and undisturbed countenances, and whose insistent use of the first person brought them to the brink of inner revelation.

From *American Humor: A Study of the National Character* (New York: Harcourt, Brace, 1931, pp. 179-86.

EDMUND WILSON

Poe as a Literary Critic

POE, at the time of his death in 1849, had had the intention of publishing a book on "The Authors of America in Prose and Verse." He had already worked over to a considerable extent the material of his articles and reviews; and the collection of critical writing printed by Griswold after his death is something between a journalistic chronicle like Bernard Shaw's dramatic notices and a selected and concentrated volume like Eliot's "The Sacred Grove."

Poe as a critic has points of resemblance both with Eliot and with Shaw. He deals vigorously and boldly with books as they come into his hands day by day, as Shaw did with the plays of the season, and manages to be brilliant and arresting even about works of no interest; he constantly insists, as Eliot does, on attempting, in the practice of this journalism, to formulate general principles. His literary articles and lectures, in fact, surely constitute the most remarkable body of criticism ever produced in the United States.

Henry James called it "probably the most complete and exquisite specimen of *provincialism* ever prepared for the edification of men." But though Poe had his share of provincialism, as all American writers did in that period, the thing that most strikes us today is his success in holding himself above it. Intellectually he stands on higher ground than any other American writer of his time. He is trying to curb the tendency of the Americans to overrate or overpraise their own books, and at the same time he is fighting a rear-guard action against the over-inflation of British reputations and the British injustice to American writers; and he has also a third battle: to break down the monopolistic instincts of the New Englanders, who tended to act as a clique and to keep out New Yorkers and Southerners. On one plane Poe grapples realistically with the practical problems of writers in the United States of that time—the copyright situation and the growth of the American magazines, with their influence on literary technique; and on another plane he is able to take in the large developments of Western literature.

With his general interest in method, he has definite ideas about the procedures in a variety of departments of literature—fiction, poetry, satire, travel, criticism. And he can be elevated, ironic, analytical, as the subject in hand requires. His prose is as taut as in his stories, but it has cast off the imagery of his fiction to become simply sharp and precise— our only first-rate classical prose of this period. His mind is a livid but incandescent shaft that is leveled at the successive objects in the American literary landscape like the searchlight on the Albany night boat that picks out the houses along the Hudson; and as there we are induced to stare at even undistinguished places which have been plucked out of the darkness into a spectral intensity of relief, so here we must read even the essays on insignificant figures whose dead features the critic makes radiant even while he is speeding them to oblivion. When we have put the whole picture together, we see it as clearly—to change the figure—as the geography of a landscape on the moon under an unattainably powerful telescope. There is no other such picture in our literature.

But Poe had tweaked the beard of Longfellow and had made people laugh at a Channing, and the lurking rancor of New England seems to have worked against the acceptance of his criticism. There is an anecdote in W. D. Howells's book, "Literary Friends and Acquaintance," which shows both the attitude of New England and the influence of this attitude on others. Howells had visited Boston for the first time when he was twenty-three, and he had gone to see Emerson in Concord. Poe had been dead ten years.

> After dinner [says Howells] we walked about in [Emerson's] "pleached garden" a little, and then we came again into his library, where I meant to linger only till I could fitly get away. He questioned me about what I had seen of Concord, and whom besides Hawthorne I had met, and when I told him only Thoreau, he asked me if I knew the poems of Mr. William Ellery Channing. I have known them since, and felt their quality, which I have gladly owned a genuine and original poetry; but I answered then truly that I knew them only from Poe's criticism: cruel and spiteful things which I should be ashamed of enjoying as I once did. "Whose criticism?" asked Emerson. "Poe's," I said again. "Oh," he cried out, after a moment, as if he had returned from a far search for my meaning, *"you mean the jingle-man."** I do not know why this should have put me to such confusion, but if I had written the criticisms myself I do not think I could have been more abashed. Perhaps I felt an edge of reproof, of admonition, in a characterization of Poe which the world will hardly agree with; though I do not agree with the world about him, myself, in its admiration. At any rate, it made an end of me for the time, and I remained as if already absent, while Emerson questioned me as to what I had written in the *Atlantic Monthly*.

That Emerson's opinion of Channing was not so very different from Poe's is shown by an entry in his journal for 1855:

*It is true that Poe had not much admired Emerson and had been rather insulting about him in A Chapter on Autography.

Ellery Channing's poetry has the merit of being genuine, and not the metrical commonplaces of the magazines, but it is painfully incomplete. He has not kept faith with the reader; 'tis shamefully insolent and slovenly. He should have lain awake all night to find the true rhyme for a verse, and he has availed himself of the first one that came; so that it is all a babyish incompleteness.

The prejudice of New England against Poe was supported by the bad reputation that had been given him by Griswold's mendacious memoir. It was not so long ago that it was possible for President Hadley of Yale to explain the refusal of the Hall of Fame to admit Poe among its immortals on the ground that he "wrote like a drunkard and a man who is not accustomed to pay his debts"; and it was only last year that Professor A. H. Quinn showed the lengths to which Griswold had gone by producing the originals of Poe's letters and printing them side by side with Griswold's falsifications.

We have often been told of Poe's criticism that it is spiteful, that it is pretentious, that it is vitiated by Poe's acceptance of the sentimental bad taste of his time. In regard to the first two of these charges it must be admitted that these essays give us unpleasant moments; they do have their queer knots and wrinkles; they are neurotic as all Poe's work is neurotic; and the distortions do here sometimes throw us off as they do not do in the stories, because it is here a question of judgment, whereas in his fiction the distortion itself is the subject of the story. It is true, as Joseph Wood Krutch has said, that there is constantly felt in Poe's criticism the same element of obsessive cruelty that inspires his tales of horror. Yet in his criticism Poe does try to hold this in check—with an occasional effect of inconsistency, in judgment as well as in tone, as when he will begin by telling us that certain passages in some book he is reviewing are among the best things of their kind to be found in contemporary writing, and then go on to pick the poet to pieces slowly, coldly, and at a length of many pages. It is also true that Poe pretends sometimes, or at least sometimes lets us infer, that he has read things he has not read. The psychology of the pretender is always a factor to be reckoned with in Poe.

The child of a fascinating actress who had died when he was two years old, he had been adopted by a Scotch merchant in Richmond, brought up as a Southern gentleman, and then cast off with no job and no money at the end of his first year of college, during which his adoptive father had failed to pay even his necessary expenses, so that he could associate, as he said, "with no students except those who were in a similar situation with myself." Poe had always been in the false situation of not being Allan's son and of knowing that in the society he was bred to his parents had been déclassés; and now he was suddenly deprived of his role of a well-heeled young Southern gentleman with prospects of inheriting a fortune, and found himself a poor man with no backing who had to survive in the American Grub Street. He had the confidence of faith in superior abilities, and the reports of his work at his English school and at the University of Virginia show that he excelled as a student. But his studies had been aborted at the same time as his social career, and a shade of the uncertainty of the "gentleman" was communicated also to the "scholar." Perhaps, also, though Poe's mind was a first-rate one, there was in him a dash of the actor who delights in elaborating a part.

Out of this consciousness of being a pretender, at any rate, with its infliction of a habitual secretiveness, came certainly Poe's love of cryptograms, his interest in inventing and solving crimes, and his indulgence in concocting and exposing hoaxes. If Poe sometimes plays unavowed tricks by cheating the reader a little about what he has written or read, the imposture is still almost as gratuitous, as innocent, and as unimportant as Stendhal's disguises and aliases and his weakness for taking ladies from the provinces through Paris and misinforming them about the public monuments. And with this we must also write off Poe's rather annoying mania of accusing his contemporaries of plagiarism—a harsh name he is in the habit of brandishing to indicate borrowings and echoes of a kind which, whether more or less abject, is usually perfectly harmless. Poe himself was certain guilty—in his imitation of Chivers, for example—of borrowings equally harmless. But these, too, touched off the pretender.

As for the charge of Poe's acquiescence in the mawkish bad taste of his period, it is deserved to only a slight degree. He more often ran counter to this taste, as when he came down on Fitz-Green Halleck; and, for the rest, his excessive enthusiasm for poets like Mrs. Osgood is attributable to the same sort of causes as, say, the praises of Bernard Shaw for the plays of Henry Arthur Jones: the writer who is potentially a master sees in the inferior writer a reflection of the kind of thing that he wants to do himself, but the possibilities of which will hardly be plain to anyone else till the master himself has made them actual.

We must recognize these warpings of Poe's line; but we must not allow them as serious impugnments of the validity of his critical work. His reading *was* wide and great, and his culture was derived from a plane of the world of thought and art which had hardly been visited by Longfellow with his patient persistent transposition of the poetry of many lands and ages into terms of his own insipidity or by Lowell with his awful cosy titles for his collections of literary essays: "My Study Windows" and "Among My Books." The truth is that literary America has always resented in Poe the very superiority which made him so quickly an international figure.

He may have been a difficult person, though certain people seem to have got on very well with him; but it seems hard to explain the virulence with which Griswold pursued him after his death and the general hostility toward him which has haunted us ever since, except on the ground that he puts us out by making so much of our culture seem second-rate. In our childhood we read "The Gold Bug" and "The Murders in the Rue Morgue," and everybody knows "Annabel Lee" and "Ulalume" and "The Bells" and "The Raven"; but Poe is not, as he is with the French and as he ought to be with us, a vital part of our intellectual equipment. It is rare that an American writer points out, as Waldo Frank once did, that Poe belongs not with the clever contrivers of fiction like O. Henry and S. S. Van Dine but, in terms of his constricted personality, with the great inquiring and versatile minds like Goethe. So that it is still worth while to insist on his value.

In the darkness of his solitary confinement Poe is still a prince.

From *The Nation*, 155 (1942), 452-53.

FLOYD STOVALL

The Achievement of Poe

JUDGED in terms of his professional career, Poe would have to be called a journalist, or perhaps a "magazinist"—a term once commonly applied to a writer contributing chiefly to magazines. For such a career he had great talent, and he achieved in it considerable success. If he had been content to be merely a popular writer, catering to the literary taste of the time, he could probably have earned far greater pecuniary rewards than he did earn in the course he followed. But he was ambitious to excel in the higher forms of literature, for which he also had great talent. His intellect was keen and fertile in ideas, his imagination was rich and active, and his sense of literary form, except in the larger conceptions of the drama, the novel, and narrative verse was almost faultless. Recognizing his limitations, he developed a theory of poetry and fiction which gave maximum support to his own genius. Within the range he allowed himself, his work, at its best, is excellent and entitles him to a place of high rank, though not the highest, in the literary pantheon. Obviously he cannot stand among the few towering figures there, with Dante, Shakespeare, and Milton, and he falls short by virtue of the narrow scope of his work of several of his elder contemporaries, like Wordsworth, whose lofty and sustained powers have raised them to eminence. His position, though in the third rank, is nevertheless honorable and secure.

By readers generally and by most critics today, Poe's tales are thought to be his best work. He is commonly given credit for inventing the detective story, which he called the story of ratiocination, and for producing two or three specimens in that genre that have never been surpassed. He also made a major contribution to the development of the short story as a distinct literary type. His own special creation was the story having but one main character and one main incident and producing in the mind of the reader a single impression or effect. He deserves more recognition than he has received for his pioneer yet brilliant use of abnormal states of mind for artistic purposes. What one most feels the absence of in his versatile display of genius and talent in fiction is the story revealing a sympathetic understanding of human nature in its normal relationships. For the style and superficial characteristics of his tales, Poe owes much to the taste of his age. In spite of that, he was perhaps the most original genius of his time. With few exceptions, every one of Poe's better tales is unique in kind; repetition, or self-imitation, that indubitable evidence of imaginative poverty, is rare indeed.

Poe was also very much of his age in the theory and practice of literary criticism, and he was best known to his contemporaries before 1845 for the discriminating insight and caustic wit of his critical reviews. He was perhaps the most important spokesman in America of the Romantic school of criticism. He had read the standard handbooks of criticism, including Aristotle's *Poetics,* and was familiar with the principles and practices followed in the British quarterlies of the early nineteenth century, but his closest intellectual ties were with Coleridge and, perhaps through him, with the German critics, A. W. and Friedrich von Schlegel, particularly the former. Like Coleridge, he believed that the artist's creative processes are analogous to the processes of God's creation; and, like Emerson, he held that beauty and truth are complementary aspects of one essential reality. Through his senses the artist has experience of the beauty of the universe; by intuition he catches glimpses of that ideal beauty which inheres in the universe as the image of its creator. It is the function of the imagination to mold sense experience into symbolic forms of ideal beauty. Poe did not subscribe, however, to the extreme organic theory that a work of art grows from the artist's mind as a tree grows, without conscious effort.

The initial impulse of conception that gives rise to artistic creation comes, it is true, from the unconscious mind as intuition, but the actual construction of the work requires the careful attention of a workman. Poe illustrates this cooperation of the conceptual and constructive faculties in "Eureka," his essay on the cyclic life of the cosmos, by saying that though Kepler guessed, or imagined, the laws of the physical universe, it required the analytical reasoning of Newton to verify and explain them. In *Marginalia* (June, 1849), he defined "Art" as "the reproduction of what the Senses perceive through the veil of the soul." To see through the veil of the soul is to see imaginatively, as Kepler saw—to grasp at once the reality of truth and beauty which lie at the heart of the phenomenal world. Once the imagination is firmly possessed of this conceptual reality, this intuition of truth and beauty, the conscious mind, the craftsman, undertakes to construct from the materials provided by the phenomenal world the image, the symbolic form, which best expresses that reality.

It was Poe's belief that every person has and uses, each in his degree, both of these faculties, the conceptual and the constructive, to which he gave the phrenological names of Ideality and Causality. It is the function of the poet to awaken in his reader through symbolic forms an intuition corresponding to his own. This intuition is accompanied by, or perhaps the result of, a state which Poe described as an excitement of the soul. To accomplish his aim, the poet must employ his constructive powers, the faculty of causality. The reader may or may not understand the process, depending upon the degree to which his own faculty of causality enables him to follow the poet's technical devices, but if he does not experience the effect intended, if his own faculty of ideality is not activated, the poet has failed. The poem can best achieve this effect if it is brief, musical, free of passion, and melancholy in tone. It must be brief because excitement by its very nature cannot be long sustained. Since the excitement is of the soul, the poem must be free of all passions of the blood, even love. The proper tone of the poem is melancholy, which Poe defines as a pleasurable sadness, because it presents an image of that ideal beauty for which the soul yearns yet knows to be unattainable in this life. Music, which is the form of beauty that most immediately affects the soul, is a quality of the poetry of words contributory to its effect of indefinite and melancholy pleasure.

A work of art created in accordance with Poe's theory will not be literally an imitation. It may, in fact, appear to be remote from actuality, vaguely suggestive of the world of experience, but not to be judged by its standard of values. This aspect of Poe's criticism, with its illustration in his poems and some of his tales, has led the advocates of art for art's sake to claim him as their spokesman. In this they are surely mistaken. Poe's famous phrases about the irreconcilable oils and waters of poetry and truth and the heresy of the didactic,[1] have too often been cited out of context. A careful reading of his essays and reviews will convince any unbiased person that Poe's restrictions on the poet refer solely to the mode of his communication. His appeal is to taste; beauty is his province. Since beauty and truth are but different aspects of the one reality, the poet may inculcate truth, as Poe himself does, by creating poems that evoke in the reader the sentiment of beauty.

Whether Poe's contribution to the theory of literary art is comparable in importance to his creative work in fiction and poetry must remain a matter of opinion. It is sufficient to say here that he developed in his own way the theories of Coleridge and his contemporary Romantics, had a fruitful influence on French poetry and criticism of the late nineteenth century, and may eventually be acknowledged to have been an important American link between the early nineteenth century and the early twentieth century in this country and abroad. It should be remembered, also, that Poe's theory of poetry is so closely identified with his poems that it cannot properly be estimated apart from them. Some of the ways in which Poe's theory is exemplified in his own verse have been indicated in Part II of this essay.

Professor Killis Campbell believed that Poe's genius was primarily that of a poet and that his greatest permanent achievement was made in poetry. Poe was himself very modest as to his accomplishments. In the Preface to *The Raven and Other Poems* he wrote:

Events not to be controlled have prevented me from making, at any time, any serious effort in what, under happier circumstances, would have been the field of my choice. With me poetry has been not a purpose, but a passion; and the passions should be held in reverence; they must not—they cannot be at will excited with an eye to the paltry compensations, or the more paltry commendations, of mankind.

Even in his youth, before he thought of journalism or faced the necessity of earning a living by his pen, his circumstances were far from happy. Yet he was able to compose and publish 1600 lines of verse before he was much past his twenty-second birthday. Although this was more than half of the verse that he cared to preserve, and indeed contains many lines of poetry as good as he ever wrote, it must not be supposed to be a fair measure of his final achievement. As I have pointed out earlier in this essay, he continued to write poetry and to improve by revision the poems he had already written. Contrary to the opinion of some of his critics, his best poems were either written or thoroughly revised during the last ten years of his life.

Poe's poems, like his tales, are notable for their original conceptions and for the technical perfection of their execution. His ear was excellent; such irregularities of meter and discordant collocations as may be found in the late poems were intentional and served a purpose more important, at the moment, than pleasing the senses. But Poe could write mellifluous verse in his later as well as in his early years, as witness "The Bells" and "Annabel Lee." Like Coleridge, he found music essential to poetry, and in the "Letter to B——,"the prefatory essay to *Poems,* 1831, which was his earliest venture in prose criticsm, he defined poetry as music combined with a pleasurable idea. There is no question as to the musical quality of his poetry. Some critics, however, have complained of the absence of ideas. In 1909 W. C. Brownell said of all Poe's writings: "They lack substance. Literature is more than an art."[2] In our time, T. S. Eliot has called Poe a gifted adolescent,[3] and Allen Tate has said that his perceptual powers remained undeveloped.[4] There is a certain amount of truth in all of these opinions; but the faults they adduce, if they exist, should be seen in the proper perspective. This perspective is provided by Poe's theory of the nature of poetry and of the function of the poet. The poet's truth is an intuition, an excitement of the soul that he called the Poetic Sentiment, and it is the product not of rational thought but of the contemplation of beauty. The only substance of beauty is form. A rational construction, such as his prose poem "Eureka" or his tales of ratiocination, may have beauty, but that beauty subsists in the consistency, the harmonious relationship, of the ideas, not in the ideas themselves.

Poe's poems can be said to lack substance only if the theory which they exemplify is wrong. If his theory is right, or if we accept that part of it which concerns the relation of beauty and truth, we must admit that his poems have the true substance of art in their power of inducing intuitions of truth in the responsive reader. Such truths are untranslatable—they cannot be expressed in terms of the intellect or of the moral sense—but they are nonetheless real to all who accept truth and beauty as of one essence. Although exponents of the doctrine of "art for art" cannot rightly claim Poe as their prophet, they may well find comfort in his poetry as in his poetic theory. Some modern poets might, in all candor, confess a greater indebtedness to Poe than they have been inclined to do. Poe was surely among the first theorists to affirm that a poem's primary value is in itself, not in what it tells us about something, whether that something be a moral or intellectual truth or some revelation of the poet himself. A poem is not a document, but a total creation; it is not a part of a world only, but a world in itself. When these matters are better understood, Poe's poetry may be more highly estimated.

Of all American writers, critics have found Poe the most difficult to categorize in a phrase. Longfellow has been depreciated as a genial sentimentalist, Emerson tolerated as a hopeful idealist, Hawthorne appreciated as a physician of souls, and Whitman hailed as a prophet of the new Eden. But Poe was neither genial nor hopeful, and he grew to look skeptically on Edens here or hereafter. In his high regard for art he was akin to Hawthorne, and in his speculative intellect he had something in common with Melville; but where in nineteenth-century America will one meet with the equal of his critical acumen, his disciplined narrative skill, or his sure feeling for verbal sounds and rhythms? On the other hand, no other American writer of the first rank lent his talent to weaker performances than some of his carping book reviews or his more grotesque attempts at humor. Three or four of his poems addressed to literary ladies do but slight credit to their author. His late poems, with their ingenious and complicated structure, have been said to "smell of the lamp." But Poe should be judged objectively on positive, not negative, evidence; in the final reckoning, his weaknesses should not be charged against his strength. One does not arrive at the true worth of a literary artist by taking an average of his work.

Perhaps Poe's greatest single literary virtue is his originality. Each of his best poems and tales, as I have said, is unique in its kind. He was not an assembly-line creator. And though his critical ideas may be largely derivative, he made them his own, enlarged them, and used them well to his own purposes. He wrote a dozen poems and nearly as many tales that approach artistic perfection. His tales, however contrived, are vivid, and the strange beauty of his poems is inimitable. Wherein lies his true genius? That would be hard to say with conviction. Any just estimate of his work must take into account his total achievement in the three fields of criticism, fiction, and poetry. In his own mind, and in the minds of a good many, though probably a minority, of his critics, he was a poet first of all and above all else. It is possible that he made his most enduring contribution to literature in the creation of a few unforgettable poems.

From "Introduction" to *The Poems of Edgar Allan Poe* (Charlottesville: The Univ. Press of Virginia), 1965, pp. xxxii-xxxvii.

1. See "The Poetic Principle."
2. *American Prose Masters* (New York: Scribner's, 1909), p. 193.
3. *From Poe to Valéry* (New York: Harcourt, Brace, 1948), p. 20.
4. *The Forlorn Demon* (Chicago: Regnery, 1953), p. 92.

Critics on Specific Works

ROY P. BASLER

The Interpretation of "Ligeia"

IN THE INTERPRETATION of "Ligeia" particularly, an understanding of the nonrational makes necessary an almost complete reversal of certain critical opinions and explanations which assume that the story is a tale of the supernatural. Clayton Hamilton's analysis of "Ligeia" in his *Manual of the Art of Fiction* (1918) is a rationalization which outdoes Poe's rationalization of "The Raven" in its attempt to show how Poe chose with mathematical accuracy just the effect and just the word which would make the perfect story of the supernatural. Unfortunately, Hamilton's basic assumptions seem obviously erroneous when he takes for granted that Ligeia is the main character, that the action of the story is concerned primarily with her struggle to overcome death, that the hero (the narrator) is "an ordinary character" who functions merely as an "eyewitness" and as a "standard by which the unusual capabilities of the central figure may be measured," and that Ligeia is "a woman of superhuman will, and her husband, a man of ordinary powers." These assumptions ignore the obvious context with its emphasis on the hero's obsession, madness, and hallucination. Actually, the story seems both aesthetically and psychologically more intelligible as a tale, not of supernatural, but rather of entirely natural, though highly phrenetic, psychological phenomena.

Perhaps the naïveté and excesses of certain psychoanalytical studies of Poe have militated against the recognition of the value of nonrational psychology in the study of Poe. At any rate, scholarly critical biographers have hesitated to credit the indubitable data of the science; and a recent critical study, A. H. Quinn's *Edgar Allan Poe: A Critical Biography* (1941), following the traditional interpretation, ignores the most obvious evidence of the nonrational theme and motivation of "Ligeia" and undertakes to analyze the story again as a tale of the supernatural. Quinn's apparent contempt for psychoanalysis and psychiatry in general, as they are applied to Poe himself, has, it seems, blinded him to the psychological patterns in "Morella" and "Berenice" as well as in "Ligeia." Although we need not consider here either the value of nonrational psychology as a means of understanding Poe's personality or the mistakes of broad assumption and overconfidence which the analysts of Poe have made, it must be recognized that, if nonrational psychology provides a better means of understanding the structure and effect of a tale like "Ligeia" and enables the reader to appreciate better what Poe accomplished as an artist, then the critic who refuses to accept nonrational psychology does so at the risk of his entire critical principle.

Let us examine the personality of the hero of "Ligeia," the narrator whose psycho-emotional experience weaves the plot. He is presented in the first paragraph as a man with an erotic obsession of long standing; his wife is presumably dead, but his idolatrous devotion to her has kept her physical beauty and her personality painfully alive in his every thought. That this devotion approaches monomania becomes more clear with every statement he makes about her. She is the acme of womanly beauty and spiritual perfection. From the time of his first acquaintance with her he has been oblivious of all but her beauty and her power over him: "I cannot, for my soul, remember how, when, or precisely where, I first became acquainted with the Lady Ligeia." Furthermore, there is his interesting admission that "I have *never known* the paternal name of her who was my friend and my betrothed, and who became the partner of my studies, and finally the wife of my bosom." In view of the fact that she was of an exceedingly ancient family and had brought him wealth "very far more, than ordinarily falls to the lot of mortals," these admissions are more than strange. Though the hero half recognizes the incongruity of his unbelievable ignorance, he dismisses it as evidence of a lover's devotion—a "wildly romantic offering on the shrine of a most passionate devotion."

Beginning with the second paragraph, we see more clearly the degree of his obsession. Although he makes much of the power of Ligeia's intellect, his imaginative preoccupation with her physical beauty is highly sensuous, even voluptuous, in its intensity. He seems to be a psychopath who has failed to find the last, final meaning of life in the coils of Ligeia's raven hair, her ivory skin, her "jetty lashes of great length," and, above all, in her eyes, "those shiny, those divine orbs!" But his imaginative desire has outrun his capabilities. Though his senses have never revealed the final meaning of the mystery which has enthralled him, his imagination refuses to accept defeat. The key to his failure is hinted in the paragraph which reveals his symbolic deification of Ligeia as a sort of personal Venus Aphrodite who personifies the dynamic urge of life itself but who, because of the hero's psychic incapacity, cannot reveal to him the "forbidden knowledge":

> There is no point, among the many incomprehensible anomalies of the science of the mind, more thrillingly exciting than the fact— never, I believe, noticed in the schools—that, in our endeavors to recall to memory something long forgotten, we often find ourselves *upon the very verge* of remembrance, without being able, in the end, to remember. And thus how frequently, in my intense scru-

tiny of Ligeia's eyes, have I felt approaching the full knowledge of their expression—felt it approaching—yet not quite be mine—and so at length entirely depart! And (strange, oh strangest mystery of all!) I found, in the commonest objects of the universe, a circle of analogies to that expression, I mean to say that, subsequently to the period when Ligeia's beauty passed into my spirit, there dwelling as in a shrine, I derived, from many experiences in the material world, a sentiment such as I felt always aroused within me by her large and luminous orbs. Yet not the more could I define that sentiment, or analyze, or even steadily view it. I recognized it, let me repeat, sometimes in the survey of a rapidly growing vine—in the contemplation of a moth, a butterfly, a chrysalis, a stream of running water. I have felt it in the ocean; in the falling of a meteor. I have felt it in the glances of unusually aged people. And there are one or two stars in heaven—(one especially, a star of the sixth magnitude, double and changeable, to be found near the large star in Lyra) in a telescopic scrutiny of which I have been made aware of the feeling. I have been filled with it by certain sounds from stringed instruments, and not unfrequently by passages from books. Among innumerable other instances, I well remember something in a volume of Joseph Glanville, which (perhaps merely from its quaintness—who shall say?) never failed to inspire me with the sentiment;—"And the will therein lieth, which dieth not. Who knoweth the mysteries of the will, with its vigor? For God is but a great will pervading all things by nature of its intentness. Man doth not yleld hlm to the angels, nor unto death utterly, save only through the weakness of his feeble will."

In this passage it is not difficult to perceive the oblique confession of inadequacy and to trace the psychological process of symbolism, which compensates for the failure of sense by apotheosis of the object of desire. Although sensuous delight leads the hero to "the very verge" of a "wisdom too divinely precious not to be forbidden," final knowledge of the secret of Ligeia's eyes is blocked by an obstacle deep within the hero's own psyche, and the insatiable imagination seeks for a realm of experience not sensual and mortal and identifies Ligeia with the dynamic power and mystery of the entire universe. She becomes not merely a woman but a goddess, through the worship of whom he "feels" that he may "pass onward to the goal of a wisdom too divinely precious not to be forbidden." There is for him, however, no possibility of fathoming the mystery which she symbolizes, though in the height of passionate adoration he feels himself to be *"upon the very verge,"* which experience he likens to that of almost but not quite recalling something from the depths of his unconscious.

This analogy of the will's inability to dictate to the unconscious and its inability to dictate to love reveals something more than the hero's vague awareness of a psychic flaw which thwarts his desire; it reveals the source of the obsession which dominates in a compensatory process his struggle to achieve by power of mind what he cannot achieve through love. The passage from Glanville is the key, the psychic formula, which he hopes may open to him the very mystery of being, his own as well as Ligeia's, in which as he conceives lies the source of the dark failure and frustration of his senses. From this psychic formula derives, then, the megalomania that he can by power of will become godlike, blending his spirit with the universal spirit of deity symbolized in the divine Ligeia, who possesses in apotheosis all the attributes of his own wish, extended in a symbolic ideal beyond the touch of mortality and raised to the absoluteness of deity—intensity in thought, passion, and sensibility; perfection in wisdom, beauty, and power of mind. It is worth noting that Poe had earlier used the name Ligeia in *Al Aaraaf* for a divinity representing much the same dynamic beauty in all nature.

But the hero's approach to power is thwarted by Ligeia's death. Just at the point when triumph seems imminent, when he feels "that delicious vista by slow degrees expanding before me, down whose long, gorgeous, and all untrodden path, I might at length pass onward to the goal of a wisdom too divinely precious not to be forbidden!" —just then Ligeia dies, because of the weakness of her own mortal will and in spite of the fervor with which the hero himself "struggled desperately in spirit with the grim Azrael."

At this point it may be noted that the obsession with the *idée fixe* expressed in the passage from Glanville begins with the hero himself and does not express Ligeia's belief. It is his will to conquer death that motivates the rest of the story, and not hers. Even when she recites the formula on her deathbed, the lines are but the echo of his wish, given in antiphonal response to the materialistic creed which she has avowed in her poem "The Conqueror Worm," which represents her philosophy and is read by the hero merely at her peremptory request. This fact is always overlooked in the rational interpretations of the story, which assume that Ligeia's struggle is the primary motivating action of the tale. Thus, in spite of her power and beauty and her passionate desire for life, "*but* for life," the earthly body of Ligeia dies—perhaps, as the obsessed hero conceives, because she has not believed in her power to conquer death. Her failure of spirit, however, is not the end. Nor is the hero's failure as he "struggled desperately in spirit with the grim Azrael" the end, but rather the beginning of the grim mania in which he is resolved to bring her back to life.

In following all that the hero says, the reader must keep constantly in mind that, if the hero is suffering from obsession, his narrative cannot be accepted merely at its face value as authentic of all the facts; and he must remember that incidents and circumstances have a primary significance in terms of the hero's mania which is often at variance with the significance which the hero believes and means to convey. This is to say that Poe's psychological effect in "Ligeia" is similar to that of later delvers in psychological complexity like Henry James, whose stories told by a narrator move on two planes. There is the story which the narrator means to tell, and there is the story which he tells without meaning to, as he unconsciously reveals himself.

Hence, the important elements in the hero's description of Ligeia are of primary significance as they reveal his feeling of psychic inadequacy, his voluptuous imagination, and his megalomania and fierce obsession with the idea that by power of will man may thwart death through spiritual love. Likewise, the narrative of the circumstances of Ligeia's death is of significance, not merely as it reveals her love of life and her struggle to live, but as it reveals the psychological crisis in which the hero's psychic shock and frustration bring on final and complete mania, the diagnostic fallacy of which is that his will is omnipotent and can bring Ligeia back to life. Up to the point of her death the hero's obsession has taken the form of adoration and worship of her person in an erotomania primarily sensual (though frustrated by a psychic flaw which he is aware of but does not understand) and hence projected into a symbolic realm of deity and forbidden wisdom. Following her death, however, his obsession becomes an intense megalomania motivated by his will to restore her to life in another body through a process of metempsychosis.

It is of particular importance that, with the beginning of the second half of the story, the reader keep in mind these two planes of meaning, for the primary significance of what the hero tells in this part is never in any circumstance the plain truth. It is rather an entirely, and obviously, fantastic representation of the facts, which justifies his obsessed psyche and proves that he has been right and Ligeia (and perhaps the gentle reader) wrong in the assumption that mortality is the common human fate—the old story of the madman who knows that he is right and the rest of the world wrong.

Thus even the hero's admission of his "incipient madness" must be recognized as the cunning condescension of the megalomaniac to the normal mind, which would not otherwise understand the excesses of his peculiar "childlike perversity" in choosing such macabre furnishings for his bridal chamber or in debauching his senses with opium—both of which "perversities" he dismisses with pseudo-naïveté as minor "absurdities." The contempt which he feels for people of normal mentality almost leads him to give himself away in his blistering question: "Where were the souls of the haughty family of the bride, when, through thirst of gold, they permitted to pass the threshold of an apartment so bedecked, a maiden and a daughter so beloved?" In other words, why could not the parents of Rowena perceive in the macabre furnishings—

the "ebony couch" with draperies of gold "spotted all over, at regular intervals, with arabesque figures. . . . of the most jetty black," the "sarcophagus of black granite," and the "endless succession of the ghastly forms which belong to the superstition of the Norman, or arise in the guilty slumbers of the monk"—why could they not perceive the obvious death chamber which he intended the bridal room to be? Likewise, one must recognize the maniacal condescension which prompts the hardly disarming naïveté with which he confesses the pleasure he derived from Rowena's dread avoidance of him in the "unhallowed hours of the first month of our marriage" and with which he testifies, "I loathed her with a hatred belonging more to demon than to man."

Perhaps he relies on this impercipiency of the normal mind to befuddle also the moral equilibrium of his audience into a sentimental acceptance of the phrenetic devotion of his spirit to the memory of Ligeia, which in his madness justifies, of course, his ghastly treatment of Rowena in terms of a pure, ethereal love for Ligeia. Thus he concludes his introductory statement in the second half of the story on a plane which, while utterly sincere in its obsessional idealism, is highly equivocal in its moral and psychological implications and reveals the fact that underlying his mad persecution of Rowena lies his frustrate desire for and worship of the lost Ligeia:

> My memory flew back (oh, with what intensity of regret!) to Ligeia, the beloved, the august, the beautiful, the entombed. I revelled in recollections of her purity, of her wisdom, of her lofty, her ethereal nature, of her passionate, her idolatrous love. Now, then, did my spirit fully and freely burn with more than all the fires of her own. In the excitement of my opium dreams (for I was habitually fettered in the shackles of the drug) I would call aloud upon her name, during the silence of the night, or among the sheltered recesses of the glens by day, as if, through the wild eagerness, the solemn passion, the consuming ardor of my longing for the departed, I could restore her to the pathway she had abandoned—ah, *could* it be forever?—upon the earth.

Up to this point in the second half of the story, the hero has unintentionally mixed a generous amount of obliquely truthful interpretation with the facts of his story; but from this point to the end he narrates events with a pseudo-objectivity that wholly, though not necessarily intentionally, falsifies their significance. He tells what he saw and heard and felt, but these things must be understood as the hallucinations of his mania, as wish-projections which arise from his obsession with the idea of resurrecting Ligeia in the body of Rowena. He tells the effects but ignores or misrepresents the causes: he wants his audience to believe that the power of Ligeia's will effected her resurrection in the body of Rowena but does not want his audience to recognize (what he himself would not) that he was the actual agent of Rowena's death and his perceptions mere hallucinations produced by obsessional desire.

In brief, it must be recognized that the hero has murdered Rowena in his maniacal attempt to restore Ligeia to life. Although his narrative of the "sudden illness" which seized Rowena "about the second month of the marriage" avoids anything which suggests a physical attempt at murder, there are unintentional confessions of deliberate psychological cruelty in the macabre furnishings of the apartment and in the weird sounds and movements designed to produce ghostly effects. The hero mentions with apparent casualness and objectivity that, "in her perturbed state of half-slumber, she spoke of sounds, and of motions, in and about the chamber of the turret, which I concluded had no origin save in the distemper of her fancy, or perhaps in the phantasmagoric influences of the chamber itself." But by his earlier confession he had calculated these "sounds" and "motions" in advance, as instruments of mental torture for the young bride, by so arranging the figured draperies as to produce optical illusions of motion and by introducing "a strong current of wind behind the draperies." He further confesses that as her dread and fear began to produce symptoms of hysteria and physical collapse he "wished to show her (what, let me confess it, I could not *all* believe) that those almost inarticulate breathings, and those gentle variations of the figures upon the wall, were but the natural effects of the customary rushing of the wind." But he did not tell her!

At this point he narrates how he became aware of a "presence" in the chamber, a supernatural agency at work. This is the wish-illusion that not he but the ghost of Ligeia, vampire-like, is preying upon the distraught and febrile body of Rowena. The details of resuscitation and relapse he wishes to believe evidence of the struggle of Ligeia's spirit to drive Rowena's spirit out of the body and to reanimate it herself. Hence arises the hallucination of the shadow on the carpet—"a faint, indefinite shadow of angelic aspect—such as might be fancied for the shadow of a shade." But, as he admits immediately, he had indulged in "an immoderate dose of opium, and heeded these things but little, nor spoke of them to Rowena." Such deprecation of his own perception is again the cunning of the maniac who must tell his story and must equally not tell it wholly, lest he spoil it by supplying evidence of a sort likely to encourage suspicion that there is something more than opiumism in his madness.

Then comes the crux of the death scene. Here, in the mélange of fact and hallucination, is *the fact* which betrays him: "I saw, or may have dreamed that I saw, fall within the goblet, as if from some invisible spring in the atmosphere of the room, three or four large drops of a brilliant and ruby colored fluid." Impatient for results and fearful that the apparent progress of Rowena's hysteria and physical collapse will not suffice, doubting the power of his will alone to effect his purpose, he has resorted to actual poison, which, however, his obsession adapts into the pattern of hallucination by perceiving that it is distilled from the atmosphere rather than dropped from a bottle held in his own hand. He cannot in his obsession recognize the bottle or the poison as physical facts, for then the power of the spirit must bow to the greater power of a merely physical drug.

The deed is accomplished, and the remainder of the narrative reveals the final stage of his mania. As the body of Rowena writhes in the throes of death, his wish takes complete command of his brain. As he watches, his mind is filled with "a thousand memories of Ligeia." The shadow on the carpet disappears, and he hears "a sob, low, gentle, but very distinct," which he "*felt*. . . . came from the bed of ebony." As evidence of returning life appears in the corpse, he feels it necessary that "some immediate exertions be made; yet the turret was altogether apart from the portion of the abbey tenanted by the servants—there were none within call—I had no means of summoning them to my aid without leaving the room for many minutes—and this I could not venture to do." With this obviously satisfactory explanation made, he relates how he struggled alone to call back "the spirit still hovering," only to fall back with a shudder and resume his "passionate waking visions of Ligeia."

Again and again the symptoms of life appear and diminish, and each time the hero testifies that he "sunk into visions of Ligeia," with the result that each period of struggle "was succeeded by I know not what of wild change in the personal appearance of the corpse," until finally his obsessed brain and senses perceive their desire-wish accomplished. The phrenetic tension of hallucination mounts in the concluding paragraph to an orgasm of psychopathic horror and wish-fulfilment in the final sentence: " 'Here, then, at least,' I shrieked aloud, 'can I never—can I never be mistaken—these are the full, and the black, and the wild eyes—of my lost love—of the lady—of the Lady Ligeia!' "

This conclusion is artistically perfect and unassailable if the story is understood to be that of a magalomaniac, a revelation of obsessional psychology and mania. If, however, the story is taken to be a rational narrative of the quasi supernatural told by a man in his right mind, the conclusion is not a conclusion but a climax, the proper denouement of which would be the corpse's reassumption of Rowena's lineaments and its final lapse into certain death, recognized this time as complete and final by the mind of the hero. Philip Pendleton Cooke, presuming the entirely rational interpretation to be the one Poe intended, called Poe's attention to this supposed weakness of the ending in a letter otherwise filled with large praise for the story's effect. Cooke's comment is as follows:

There I was shocked by a violation of the ghostly proprieties—so to speak—and wondered how the lady Ligeia—a wandering essence— could, in quickening *the body of the Lady Rowena* (such is the idea) become suddenly the visible, bodily Ligeia.

Poe's answer takes full cognizance of the justice of Cooke's criticism and tacitly admits the rational interpretation to be the one he intended, making the somewhat lame excuse that

it was necessary, since "Morella" was written, to modify "Ligeia." I was forced to be content with a sudden half-consciousness, on the part of the narrator, that Ligeia stood before him. One point I have not fully carried out—I should have intimated that the *will* did not perfect its intention—there should have been a relapse—a final one —and Ligeia (who had only succeeded in so much as to convey an idea of the truth to the narrator) should be at length entombed as Rowena—the bodily alterations having gradually faded away.

It is possible that Poe meant in this statement merely to bow to Cooke's praise and accept a criticism which completely misses the primary significance of the entire story, in order to avoid the necessity of explaining to an admirer the painful truth that he had missed the point. Poe was avid for the praise that came all too seldom, and he may have avoided controversy with his appreciative correspondent somewhat out of gratitude. That he could not have held seriously or for long the opinion that the story needed an added denouement seems obvious from the fact that, although he made careful and detailed revisions of the story afterward, he did not alter the nature of the conclusion. That he would have done so without hesitation had he actually believed the conclusion defective, we may be sure from his indefatigable practice of revising his favorite pieces even in the minor details which did not fulfil his wishes.

There seem to be two alternatives here: either Poe meant the story to be read as Cooke read it, and failed to provide the sort of conclusion which he admitted to be necessary, or he meant it to be read approximately as we have analyzed it, and merely bowed to Cooke's criticism out of gratitude for appreciation. Possibly there is a third alternative, however, one which is not incompatible with Poe's genius. Perhaps the intention in the story was not entirely clear and rationalized in his own mind, preoccupied as he was with the very ideas and obsessions which motivate the hero of the story. Anyone who has studied Poe's rationalization of "The Raven" must recognize that in its *post hoc* reasoning Poe entirely ignores the obvious psycho-emotional motivation of his own creative process. In his offhand and casual comments on his writings, however, he sometimes recognizes the essentially "unconscious" source of his compositions. An example of this recognition is his comment written in a copy of the *Broadway Journal* which he sent to Mrs. Sarah Helen Whitman:

> The poem ["To Helen"—of 1848] which I sent you contained all the events of a *dream* which occurred to me soon after I knew you. Ligeia was also suggested by *a dream*—observe the *eyes* in both tale and poem.

Thus, in this third alternative we may perceive the possibility that as an artist Poe produced in "Ligeia" a story which faithfully depicts the functioning of both rational and nonrational processes in a mind obsessed by a psychopathic desire that becomes the diagnostic of a megalomania in which power of will (wish) is conceived as overcoming the physical fact of death and the grave, but that Poe was not entirely clear in his own mind concerning the nonrational logic of the unconscious which he used as an artist depicting his hero as conceived in a dream and, hence, accepted Cooke's criticism as justified, even though in his own feeling he recognized the "truth" and appropriateness of the conclusion as he had written it, in part, at least, out of his own unconscious. Poe's penciled comment on the manuscript copy of one of his later poems, as quoted by Mrs. Sarah Helen Whitman, is similarly indicative of the source of his artistic certainty:

> "All that I have here expressed was actually present to me. Remember the mental condition which gave rise to 'Ligeia'—recall the passage of which I spoke, and observe the coincidence. . . . I regard these visions," he says, "even as they arise, with an awe which in some measure moderates or tranquillizes the ecstacy—I so regard them through a conviction that this ecstacy, in itself, is of a character supernal to the human nature—*is a glimpse of the spirit's outer world.*"

Thus, when he came to revise the story, his artistic sense, rooted deeply in his own unconscious processes (or, if one chooses, in "the spirit's outer world"), did not permit the alteration of the conclusion to fit an interpretation essentially superficial and incomplete in its perception of the psychological origin of the story. Had Poe understood as much of the nonrational processes of the psyche as does even the layman of today, he might have written as a critic a reply to Cooke that would have outdone "The Philosophy of Composition" in logical analysis of the creation of a work of art out of both rational and nonrational mental processes, but it is not likely that he could have written as an artist a more effective psychological story than "Ligeia."

The merits of this analysis must, of course, stand or be dismissed on the evidence in the context of the story itself, and the evidence in this case is—what it is not in the case of Poe's personality—complete. The hero of the story either is or is not to be completely trusted as a rational narrator whose account can be accepted with the meaning which he wishes it to have, and Poe either does or does not give the reader to understand which point of view he must take. To me, at least, Poe makes obvious the fact of the hero's original obsession in the first half of the story and his megalomania in the second half. The concluding paragraph remains aesthetically as utterly incomprehensible to me as it was to Philip Pendleton Cooke, if the story is merely a story of the supernatural designed to produce an impression. And I cannot think that Poe, fully aware of the justice of Cooke's criticism in that view, would have left the denouement as it was originally written without believing that there was more artistic verisimilitude in the story as he had created it than there was in the story as Cooke had interpreted it.

From *College English,* 5 (1944), 364-72.

WILLIAM BYSSHE STEIN

The Twin Motif in
"The Fall of the House of Usher"

SINCE POE'S PRACTICE of the short story is obviously based upon
the principle of scrupulous execution—the studied manipulation of "a
certain *single effect*"—the function of structural details would seem to
warrant the most careful critical examination. But this kind of attention has not generally been given to "The Fall of the House of Usher"
(nor, for that matter, to the other tales of emotional and mental perversion). Its distinctive unity of plot and tone has excited little more than
perfunctory comment, and the crucial importance of the twin motif in
the preconceived design has virtually been ignored. Yet the Gothic
convention of the common fate of twins is the chief vehicle both of
Poe's effect of terror and of his psychological rationalization of the
terror.

The "invented" action and ambience of the story, while seemingly
mechanical modes of suspense, are actually diversiform projections of
Roderick's compulsive absorption with the appalling folk superstition
about twins, what he calls "the grim phantasm." Indeed, the narrator's
report of background, scene, and incident is always focussed on the
implications of Madeline's illness. The opening description of the "sick-
ening" decay of the external setting symbolically figures the hero's
physical and mental condition. However, in the reminiscence which
immediately follows, this state is connected with the "undeviating"
male line of descent in the Usher race, a hereditary deficiency directly
affecting the sister's future destiny. In present time this emphasis is
extended by the introduction of the sinister physician who is treating
her mysterious disease. The succeeding symptoms of Roderick's "acute
bodily illness" and "mental disorder" are part of this same pattern of
relations, for he despairingly associates "the nature of his malady" with
her sickness: "He admitted, however, although with hesitation, that
much of the peculiar gloom which thus afflicted him could be traced to
a more natural and far more palpable origin—to the severe and long-
continued illness—indeed to the evidently approaching dissolution—of a
tenderly beloved sister. . . . 'Her decease,' he said, with a bitterness
which I can never forget, 'would leave him . . . the last of the ancient
race of the Ushers.' " Confirming evidence that the twin motif controls
the development of suspense is found in Poe's elucidation of Roderick's
inexplicable reactions to Madeline's death and subsequent burial in the

underground vault, actually the frightful apprehensions attending his conviction that he too ought to be dead: "There were times, indeed, when I thought his unceasingly agitated mind labored with some oppressive secret, to divulge which he struggled for the necessary courage." Structurally, the later revelation of the significance of this ravaging obsession is made to coincide with the climactic moment of terror, Madeline's fateful resurrection.

Her miraculous escape from the closed coffin and the locked tomb is, of course, a *tour de force* of Gothic sensationalism. But to limit its meaning to this view alone is to ignore its symbolic function, for the incident is the chief agency of the psychological disclosures in the story. Though Roderick's dissociation of personality has countless external correlatives, from the fissure in the house to his physical and intellectual idiosyncrasies, his psychic condition, in the casual sense, cannot be clearly understood unless it is directly related to the illness of his twin sister. Madeline, like the other William Wilson, Ligeia, and the pursued criminal in "The Man in the Crowd" (a story often misread because the pursuer, the first-person narrator, is not recognized as the protagonist), is a visible embodiment of the alter ego. She stands for the emotional or instinctive side of her brother's personality which has stagnated under the domination of the intellect (here the tarn is a dramatic image). But as attested by the interior poem, a synecdoche of his conflict and its outcome, these repressed feelings will ultimately revolt against such tyranny. This turn of events is symbolized in the disappearance of the house and its occupant (the head and its monarch "Thought" in the poem) into the storm-tossed waters of the tarn. In sum, the outraged unconscious swallows up all conscious authority, and Roderick is rendered completely insane. As Madeline escapes her death-in-life confinement on the literal level of action, on the psychological level the instincts (or alter ego) attain their release. Thus the two levels of reality in the tale are brought into perfect conjunction, and the twin motif is the structural device that controls the final synthesis of form and, inevitably, of tone.

From *Modern Language Notes,* 75 (1960), 109-11.

JOSEPH PATRICK ROPPOLO

Meaning and "The Masque of the Red Death"

THOSE WHO SEEK guidance in interpreting Edgar Allan Poe's "The Masque of the Red Death" are doomed to enter a strange world, as confused and confusing as a Gothic Wonderland and in some respects as eerie as the blighted house of Roderick Usher. Their guides will be old critics, New Critics, scholars, biographers, enthusiasts, dilettantes, journalists, hobbyists, anthologists, medical men, psychologists, and psychoanalysts. From these the seekers will learn that Prince Prospero is Poe himself and that "The Masque" is therefore autobiography; that Poe never presents a moral; that "The Masque" is an allegory and must therefore teach a lesson; that there is indeed a moral; that there are unnumbered morals; that there is no message or meaning; that there is a message; that the message is quite obvious and understandable; and that the meaning of the message transcends human understanding. In the pages that follow I should like to tour, briefly, the tangled world of the critics of "The Masque of the Red Death" and then to explore "The Masque" with the best of all possible guides—Poe himself.

I

A representative of the psychological guides and of the group which sees no meaning in "The Masque of the Red Death" is Albert Mordell, whose book, *The Erotic Motive in Literature,* widely read since 1919, was reissued in 1962 with a new section on Poe. Mordell writes blithely of Poe's "Loss of Breadth" and of a character named Roger Usher who, "like Poe, had been disappointed in love, and probably also drank."[1] To Mordell, Poe was not only a frustrated lover and a drunkard; he was also a sadist and a masochist, a man who suffered from "a damming of the libido" and who was "so absorbed in his dreams that he never tried to take an interest in reality. Hence," Mordell concludes, "we will find no moral note in Poe's work"—with the single exception of "William Wilson."[2]

In sharp contrast, Vincent Buranelli argues that Poe "was no sadist, no masochist, no pervert, no rake," but was instead "the sanest of our writers"—that he was, in fact, "America's greatest writer, and the American writer of greatest significance in world literature."[3] Yet, oddly, Buranelli finds himself aligned with Mordell when he, too, asserts sweepingly that "Poe does not touch morality"; and he finds himself involved in something of a contradiction when he describes "The Masque of the Red Death" as "an allegory representing Death itself as one of the *dramatis personae*."[4] Allegory, typically, is meaningful and moral, but Buranelli does not elaborate upon his statement; nor does he reconcile Poe's well-known detestation of allegory with Poe's use of it in one of his acknowledged masterpieces.[5]

Joseph Wood Krutch, who saw Poe as incompetent, sexless, and mad, but nevertheless marked by genius, dismissed "The Masque of the Red Death" as "merely the most perfect [sic] description of that fantastic *décor* which [Poe] had again and again imagined."[6] Edward H. Davidson remarks on the paucity of "fact and information" in the piece and reveals that "tone and movement are all."[7] Commenting at greater length, David M. Rein summarizes the narrative and adds that

> The prince, of course, represents Poe, once again as a young man of wealthy and distinguished family. Here Poe dreamed of escape from the harsh world, where such evils as the plague were dominant—escape into a secluded place of pleasure he himself designed. But like so many of Poe's fantasies, this dream world would not remain intact; the imaginary refuge, in spite of all precautions, was invaded by Death, whose merest look destroyed him. It may be significant, too, that all in this company fell back to avoid encountering the gruesome figure. The prince alone, unwilling to await the stranger's pleasure, went forth to pursue him. Does not Poe here once again in fantasy, impatiently seek a danger that seems inescapable?[8]

Avoiding the pitfall of imagining Poe's ratiocinative mind losing control of a carefully imagined dream world, Killis Campbell, among others, contented himself with seeking sources and with attempting to ground the fantasy of "The Masque of the Red Death" in fact. In *The Mind of Poe and Other Studies,*[9] Campbell points out that Poe was "pretty clearly indebted to William Harrison Ainsworth's *Old Saint Paul's*" and then cites an account by N. P. Willis in the *New York Mirror* of June 2, 1832, in which Willis describes a Parisian ball featuring "The Cholera Waltz," "The Cholera Galopade," and, most pertinently, a masked figure representing the cholera itself. Willard Thorp, in *A Southern Reader,*[10] makes the identity of Poe's Red Death positive: it is, Thorpe says, "undoubtedly the cholera, newly arrived in America"; Poe colors it red to distinguish it from the Black Death—the bubonic plague.[11] In a more literary vein, numerous scholars have pointed out the use of the words "red plague" by Shakespeare in *The Tempest* (I.ii.364). without, however, making useful applications to Poe's "Masque."

Arthur Hobson Quinn is among those who believe that "The Masque of the Red Death" contains a moral or a message (he uses the terms interchangeably). "With a restraint that is one of the surest marks of genius," Quinn says, "Poe gives no hint of the great moral the tale tells to those who can think. For the others, he had no message."[12] Whereupon Quinn leaves his reader to place himself among the thinkers or, unhappily, among the non-thinkers, disdaining to make explicit or even to suggest the "great moral" which Poe shields behind his "Masque."

Patrick F. Quinn agrees that "The Masque of the Red Death" is "one of the few serious moral tales that Poe ever wrote,"[13] but he, too, spares the reader the embarrassment of having the moral or morals pointed out to him. Others are less reticent, and their interpretations tend to fall into the familiar pattern of the *memento mori*. Typical are Frances Winwar and Norman Foerster.

To Frances Winwar, "The Masque of the Red Death" is "a compelling fantasy in scarlet and black where every effect stresses the inevitability of final dissolution. . . . "[14] Foerster notes that red is "Poe's most frequent color" and sees in it "the horror of blood." To Foerster "The Masque of the Red Death" is a richly vivid contrast between life and death. Setting dominates, and "magnificence and voluptuousness heighten the sense of worldly pleasure till the heart of life beats feverishly—and stops." The clock symbolizes the processes of time—both life and death.[15]

Three critics, Walter Blair, Harry Levin, and Marie Bonaparte, go far beyond the routine. To Blair, as to many others, there is "allegorical signification" in the seven rooms, which, "progressing from east to west—from blue to black—connote the seven ages of man from the blue of the dawn of life to the black of its night." The clock is, of course, Time; the masked figure is the Red Death; and the revelers are the living, "who seek to bar out and forget death by being gay and carefree," only to discover that death must inevitably conquer all humanity. So far, the critic is in the mainstream of interpretation. But Blair, more perceptive than most, refuses to confine "The Masque of the Red Death" to this moral. The closing note of the last paragraph is "inconsistent with such a meaning"; and Poe, a lover of ambiguity, would probably argue, Blair says, that "The Masque" is "suggestive of implications which cannot be made explicit this side of eternity."[16] Harry Levin makes the venture. "The closing note, echoed from the pseudo-Miltonic last line of Pope's *Dunciad*," Levin says, "predicates a reduction of cosmos to chaos"[17]—a challenging and, I hope to show, a fruitful bit of speculation.

It is left to Princess Bonaparte to lift "The Masque of the Red Death" from the limited realm of allegory to the expansive kingdom of myth. But, having placed "The Masque" among "typical" Oedipus stories, along with "The Cask of Amontillado," the Princess bogs down in a morass of conflicting Freudian symbols. The Prince, of course, is Oedipus, the son. The masked figure is the father. The castle of seven rooms is the body of the mother. The uplifted dagger is a phallus. The dropped dagger is the castrated phallus. And the Red Death—whether father-figure or something beyond that—is both death and castration. [18] We are back in the weird and wonderful world of Albert Mordell, who, not surprisingly, admits owing a great debt to Princess Bonaparte.

Of all the critics mentioned, Blair is the most detailed and in many ways the most convincing. Foerster's brief statement, too, almost compels belief. But I should like to suggest that neither goes far enough. Foerster evades consideration of Poe's final paragraph. Blair acknowledges that paragraph—vitally important because of its position—but leaves all attempts at its clarification to the other side of eternity. If Foerster's evasion is justified (and Levin's remark indicates that it is not), then Poe has failed to follow one of his own precepts, that "In the whole composition there should be no word written, of which the tendency, direct or indirect, is not to be the one pre-established design." [19] And if Blair is correct, then Poe must have sprinkled his page with more than a grain of salt when he wrote that "Every work of art should contain within itself all that is requisite for its own comprehension." [20] I do not believe that Poe was less than a remarkably skilled craftsman, nor do I believe that his critical dicta were deliberate jests. I should like to take Poe at his word in both quoted statements and, with both steadily in mind, study "The Masque of the Red Death" to see what it yields.

II

In Poe's imaginative prose, beginnings unfailingly are important. "The Masque of the Red Death" begins with these three short sentences:

> The "Red Death" had long devastated the country. No pestilence had ever been so fatal or so hideous. Blood was its Avatar and its seal—the redness and horror of blood.

On one level, the reader is introduced to a disease, a plague, with hideous and terrifying symptoms, a remarkably rapid course, and inevitable termination in death. But Poe's heaviest emphasis is on blood, not as sign or symptom, but as avatar and seal. A seal is something that confirms or assures or ratifies. The appearance—the presence—of blood is confirmation or assurance of the existence of the Red Death or, more broadly, of Death itself. As avatar, blood is the incarnation, the bodily representation, of the Red Death. It is, further, something god-like, an eternal principle, for in Hindu myth, the word "avatar" referred to the descent of a god, in human form, tò earth. Further, "avatar" can be defined as "a variant phase or version of a continuing entity." [21] A second level thus emerges: blood represents something invisible and eternal, a ruling principle of the universe. That principle, Poe seems to suggest, is death.

But is it? The Red Death, Poe tells us, "had long devastated the country." And then: "No pestilence had ever been so fatal"—surely a remarkable second sentence for a man so careful of grammar and logic as Poe. Is or is not the Red Death a pestilence? And does the word "fatal" permit of comparison? I should like to suggest that here Poe is being neither ungrammatical nor even carefully ambiguous, but daringly clear. The Red Death is not a pestilence, in the usual sense; it is unfailingly and universally fatal, as no mere disease or plague can be; and blood is its guarantee, its avatar and seal. Life itself, then, is the Red Death, the one "affliction" shared by all mankind. [22]

For purposes of commenting on life and of achieving his single effect, Poe chooses to emphasize death. He is aware not only of the brevity of all life and of its inevitable termination but also of men's isolation: blood, the visible sign of life, is, Poe says, "the pest ban which shuts him out from the aid and sympathy of his fellow man." In the trap of life and in his death, every man *is* an island. If there is a mutual bond, it is the shared horror of death.

Out of the chaos that has "long devastated" his dominions, Prince Prospero creates a new and smaller world for the preservation of life. A kind of demi-god, Prospero can "create" his world, and he can people it; but time (the ebony clock) exists in his new world, and he is, of course, deluded in his belief that he can let in life and shut out death. Prospero's world of seven rooms, without "means [either] of ingress or egress," is a microcosm, as the parallel with the seven ages of man indicates, and its people are eminently human, with their predilection for pleasure and their susceptibility to "sudden impulses of despair or frenzy." In their masquerade costumes, the people are "in fact, a multitude of dreams," but they are fashioned like the inhabitants of the macrocosmic world. Many are beautiful, but many also are bizarre or grotesque. Some are wanton; some are "arabesque figures with unsuited limbs and appointments"; some are terrible, some are disgusting, and some are "delirious fancies such as the madman fashions" (and Prospero, the demi-god, for all his "fine eye for colors and effects," may indeed be mad). But all of them are life, and in six of the seven apartments "the heart of life" beats "feverishly." And even here, by deliberate use of the word "feverishly," Poe links life with disease and death.

The seventh apartment is not the room of death; death occurs in fact in each of the rooms. It is, however, the room in which the reminders of death are strongest, and it is the room to which all must come who traverse the preceding six. Death's colors, red and black, are there; and there the ebony clock mercilessly measures Time, reminding the revel-

ers hour after hour that life, like the course of the Red Death, is short.
When the clock strikes the dreaded hour of twelve, the revelers
become aware suddenly of the presence of a masked figure which none
has noted before:

> The figure was tall and gaunt, and shrouded from head to foot in
> the habiliments of the grave. The mask which concealed the visage
> was made so nearly to resemble the countenance of a stiffened
> corpse that the closest scrutiny must have had difficulty in detect-
> ing the cheat. And yet all this might have been endured, if not
> approved, by the mad revellers around. But the mummer had gone
> so far as to assume the type of the Red Death. His vesture was
> dabbled in *blood*—and his broad brow, with all the features of the
> face, was besprinkled with the scarlet horror.

Poe does not indicate in which room the awareness of the masked
figure occurred first, but Prince Prospero sees this blood-sprinkled horror in the blue, or easternmost, room, which is usually associated with
birth, rather than with death. The figure moves then through each of
the apartments, and Prospero follows, to meet his own death in the
room of black and red.

Not once does Poe say that the figure is the Red Death. Instead,
"this new presence" is called "the masked figure," "the stranger," "the
mummer," "this spectral image," and "the intruder." He is "shrouded"
in "the habiliments of the grave," the dress provided by the living for
their dead and endowed by the living with all the horror and terror
which they associate with death. The mask, fashioned to resemble "the
countenance of a stiffened corpse," is but a mask, a "cheat." And all
this, we are told, "might have been borne" had it not been for the
blood, that inescapable reminder to life of the inevitability of death.
The intruder is, literally, "The *Mask* of the Red Death,"[23] not the
plague itself, nor even—as many would have it—the all-inclusive representation of Death.

There is horror in the discovery that "the grave-cerements and
corpse-like mask" are "untenanted by any tangible form," but the
horror runs more deeply than the supernatural interpretation allows, so
deeply in fact that it washes itself clean to emerge as Truth. Blood, Poe
has been saying, is (or is symbolic of) the life force; but even as it
suggests life, blood serves as a reminder of death.[24] Man himself invests
death with elements of terror, and he clothes not death but the terror
of death in garb of his own making—"the habiliments of the grave"—
and then runs, foolishly, to escape it or, madly, to kill it, mistaking the
mummer, the cheat, for death itself. The fear of death can kill: Prospero attempts to attack the masked figure and fails; but when man's
image of death is confronted directly, it is found to be nothing. The

vestments are empty. The intruder in "The Masque of the Red Death" is, then, not the plague, not death itself, but man's creation, his self-aroused and self-developed fear of his own mistaken concept of death.

Death is nevertheless present, as pervasive and as invisible as eternal law. He is nowhere and everywhere, not only near, about, and around man, but in him. And so it is, at last, that, having unmasked their unreasoning fear, the revelers acknowledge the presence of the Red Death. One by one, the revelers die—as everything endowed with life must; and, with the last of them, time, which is measured and feared only by man, dies, too.[25]

Poe might have stopped there, just as he might have ended "The Raven" with the sixteenth stanza. The narrative is complete, and there are even "morals" or "lessons" for those who demand them. But, as Poe says in "The Philosophy of Composition,"

> in subjects so handled, however skilfully, or with however vivid an array of incident, there is always a certain hardness or nakedness, which repels the artistical eye. Two things are invariably required—first, some amount of complexity, or more properly, adaptation; and, secondly, some amount of suggestiveness—some undercurrent, however indefinite, of meaning.

To achieve complexity and suggestiveness, Poe added two stanzas to "The Raven." To "The Masque of the Red Death" he added two sentences: "And the flames of the tripods expired. And Darkness and Decay and the Red Death held illimitable dominion over all."

"Let there be light" was one of the principles of Creation; darkness, then, is a principle of Chaos. And to Poe Chaos is synonymous with Nothingness, "which, to all finite perception, Unity must be." Decay occurs as matter "expels the ether" to return to or to sink into Unity. Prince Prospero's world, created out of a chaos ruled by the Red Death, returns to chaos, ruled by the trinity of Darkness and Decay and the Red Death. But, it will be remembered, Prince Prospero's world came into being *because of* the Red Death, which, although it includes death, is the principle of life. In Chaos, then, is the promise of new lives and of new worlds which will swell into existence and then, in their turn, subside into nothingness in the eternal process of contraction and expansion which Poe describes in "Eureka."[26]

There are "morals" implicit and explicit in this interpretation of "The Masque of the Red Death," but they need not be underlined here. Poe, who had maintained in his "Review of Nathaniel Hawthorne's *Twice-Told Tales*" that "Truth is often, and in very great degree, the aim of the tale," was working with a larger, but surely not entirely inexpressible, truth than can be conveyed in a simple "Poor Richard" maxim; and in that task, it seems to me, he transcends the tale (into which classification most critics put "The Masque of the Red Death") to create a prose which, in its free rhythms, its diction, its compression, and its suggestion, approaches poetry.[27]

The ideas that were haunting Poe when he published "Eureka" were already haunting him in 1842, when he published "The Masque of the Red Death," and what emerged was not, certainly, a short story; nor was it, except by the freest definition, a tale. For either category, it is deficient in plot and in characterization. Instead, "The Masque of the Red Death" combines elements of the parable and of the myth. Not as explicit or as pointedly allegorical always as the parable, "The Masque of the Red Death" nevertheless can be (and has been) read as a parable of the inevitability and the universality of death; but it deals also with the feats of a hero or demigod—Prospero—and with Poe's concepts of universal principles, and it has the mystery and the remoteness of myth. What Poe has created, then, is a kind of mythic parable, brief and poetic, of the human condition, of man's fate, and of the fate of the universe.

From *Tulane Studies in English,* 13 (1963), 59-69.

1. See Albert Mordell, *The Erotic Motive in Literature* (New York: Collier Books, 1962), pp. 173-175. Apparently Mordell was unaware of his remarkable Freudian slip in re-naming Roderick Usher. The reference to "Loss of Breath" occurs on p. xxi. It is, perhaps (hopefully), a printer's error.

2. Mordell, pp. 174, 175, and (especially) 177.

3. Vincent Buranelli, *Edgar Allan Poe* (New York: Twayne Publishers, Inc., 1961), pp. 11, 63, and 133.

4. Buranelli, pp. 72, 73.

5. Buranelli himself (p. 125) refers to the fact that Poe "detested . . . allegory."

6. Joseph Wood Krutch, *Edgar Allan Poe: A Study in Genius* (New York: Alfred A. Knopf, 1926), p. 77.

7. Edward H. Davidson, *Poe: A Critical Study* (Cambridge: The Belknap Press of Harvard University Press, 1957), p. 154.

8. David M. Rein, *Edgar A. Poe: The Inner Pattern* (New York: Philosophical Library, 1960), p. 33.

9. (Cambridge, Mass.: Harvard University Press, 1933), p. 177 and note.

10. (New York: Alfred A. Knopf, 1955), p. 656n.

11. To my knowledge no one has pointed out that cholera generally—both in the popular mind and etymologically—has been and is associated with yellow.

12. Arthur Hobson Quinn, *Edgar Allan Poe: A Critical Biography* (New York: D. Appleton-Century Company, Inc., 1941), p. 331.

13. Patrick F. Quinn, *The French Face of Edgar Allan Poe* (Carbondale: Southern Illinois University Press, 1957), p. 115.

14. Frances Winwar, *The Haunted Palace: A Life of Edgar Allan Poe* (New York: Harper & Brothers, Publishers, 1959) p. 227.

15. Norman Foerster, ed., *American Poetry and Prose* (Boston: Houghton Mifflin Company, 1957), I, 424.

16. Walter Blair, "Poe's Conception of Incident and Tone in the Tale," *Modern Philology,* XLI (May, 1944), 228-240, especially pp. 239, 240.

17. Harry Levin, *The Power of Blackness: Hawthorne, Poe, Melville* (New York: Vintage Books, 1960), p. 150.

18. Marie Bonaparte, *The Life and Works of Edgar Allan Poe: A Psychoanalytic Approach* (London: Imago Publishing Co., Ltd., 1949), pp. 513, 515. Princess Bonaparte's conclusion is interesting: for Prospero, "as for Poe," she says, ". . . sensual delight had no genital expression."

19. In Poe's "Review of Nathaniel Hawthorne's *Twice-Told Tales.*"

20. In Poe's essay, "Longfellow's Ballads."

21. Reference to the *OED* will show that all meanings given here for *seal* and *avatar* were current in Poe's time.

22. "For the life of all flesh is the blood thereof" (*Leviticus,* 17:14). Poe knew the Bible well, and references to and quotations from the Bible are frequent in his works. In *Biblical Allusions in Poe* (New York: The Macmillan Company, 1928), William Mentzel Forrest says that Poe's views on death are "essentially Biblical" and points out that "Throughout the Old Testament death is looked upon not from the religious but from the natural viewpoint, as something to which all life is subject in harmony with the great laws of change" (p. 58).

23. Poe's original title for this short prose piece, when it appeared in *Graham's Lady and Gentleman's Magazine* in May, 1842, was "The Mask of the Red Death. A Fantasy."

24. Charles O'Donnell, in "From Earth to Ether: Poe's Flight into Space," *PMLA,* LXXVII (March, 1962), pp. 88, 89, makes much the same point in his discussion of *The Narrative of Arthur Gordon Pym.* O'Donnell speaks of blood as "the life force" and as "suggestive of life, mystery, suffering, terror—in general of the human situation."

25. "The angel which I saw stand upon the sea and upon the earth . . . sware . . . that there should be time no longer" (Revelation 10:5, 6).

26. Poe's theories of the universe, including his theory of the identity of Unity and Nothingness, are explained in detail in "Eureka." Also pertinent is Poe's statement in "Eureka" that "In the Original Unity of the First Thing lies the Secondary Cause of All Things, with the Germ of their Inevitable Annihilation."

27. Poe calls "Eureka" a prose poem, "Shadow" a parable, and "Silence" a fable. Both "Shadow" and "Silence" have many of the qualities of prose poetry. According to Buranelli (p. 113), Poe believed that "prose poetry is genuine poetry; intellectually impoverished rhyme is not." Blair (p. 238) also notes that the indefiniteness and suggestiveness of "The Masque of the Red Death" are "calculated to elevate the soul"—and elevation of the soul is, according to Poe, the function of poetry.

E. ARTHUR ROBINSON

Poe's "The Tell-Tale Heart"

POE'S "THE TELL-TALE HEART" consists of a monologue in which an accused murderer protests his sanity rather than his innocence. The point of view is the criminal's, but the tone is ironic in that his protestation of sanity produces an opposite effect upon the reader. From these two premises stem multiple levels of action in the story. The criminal, for example, appears obsessed with defending his physic self at whatever cost, but actually his drive is self-destructive since successful defense upon either implied charge—of murder or of criminal insanity—automatically involves admission of guilt upon the other.

Specifically, the narrator bases his plea upon the assumption that madness is incompatible with systematic action, and as evidence of his capacity for the latter he relates how he has executed a horrible crime with rational precision. He reiterates this argument until it falls into a pattern: "If still you think me mad, you will think so no longer when I describe the wise precautions I took for concealment of the body."[1] At the same time he discloses a deep psychological confusion. Almost casually he admits lack of normal motivation: "Object there was none. Passion there was none. I loved the old man." Yet in spite of this affection he says that the idea ot murder "haunted me day and night." Since such processes of reasoning tend to convict the speaker of madness, it does not seem out of keeping that he is driven to confession by "hearing" reverberations of the still-beating heart in the corpse he has dismembered, nor that he appears unaware of the irrationalities in his defense of rationality.

At first reading, the elements of "The Tell-Tale Heart" appear simple: the story itself is one of Poe's shortest; it contains only two main characters, both unnamed, and three indistinguishable police officers; even the setting of the narration is left unspecified. In the present study my object is to show that beneath its narrative flow the story illustrates the elaboration of design which Poe customarily sought, and also that it contains two of the major psychological themes dramatized in his longer works.

It is important to note that Poe's theory of art emphasizes development almost equally with unity of effect. There must be, he insists, "a repetition of purpose," a "dropping of the water upon the rock;"[2] thus he calls heavily upon the artist's craftsmanship to devise thematic modifications of the "preconceived effect." A favorite image in his stories is that of arabesque ornamentation with repetitive design. In "The Tell-Tale Heart" one can distinguish several such recurring devices filling out the "design" of the tale, the most evident being what the narrator calls his "over acuteness of the senses." He incorporates this physical keenness into his plea of sanity: ". . . why *will* you say that I am mad? The disease has sharpened my senses—not destroyed, not dulled them. Above all was the sense of hearing acute." He likens the sound of the old man's heart to the ticking of a watch "enveloped in cotton" and then fancies that its terrified beating may arouse the neighbors. His sensitivity to sight is equally disturbing, for it is the old man's eye, "a pale blue eye, with a film over it," which first vexed him and which he seeks to destroy. Similar though less extreme powers are ascribed to the old man. For example, the murderer congratulates himself that not even his victim could have detected anything wrong with the floor which has been replaced over the body, and earlier he imagines the old man, awakened by "the first slight noise," listening to determine whether the sound has come from an intruder or "the wind in the chimney." Variations such as these give the sensory details a thematic significance similar to that of the "morbid acuteness of the senses" of Roderick Usher in "The Fall of the House of Usher" or the intensity with which the victim of the Inquisition hears, sees, and smells his approaching doom in "The Pit and the Pendulum."

These sensory data provide the foundation for an interesting psychological phenomenon in the story. As the characters listen in the darkness, intervals of strained attention are prolonged until the effect resembles that of slow motion. Thus for seven nights the madman enters the room so "very, very slowly" that it takes him an hour to get his head through the doorway; as he says, "a watch's minute-hand moves more quickly than did mine." When on the eighth night the old man is alarmed, "for a whole hour I did not move a muscle." Later he is roused to fury by the man's terror, but "even yet," he declares, "I refrained and kept still. I scarcely breathed." On different nights both men sit paralyzed in bed, listening for terrors real or imagined. After the murder is completed, "I placed my hand upon the heart and held it there many minutes." In the end it seems to his overstrained nerves that the police officers linger inordinately in the house, chatting and smiling, until he is driven frantic by their cheerful persistence.

This psychological process is important to "The Tell-Tale Heart" in two ways. First, reduplication of the device gives the story structural power. Poe here repeats a dominating impression at least seven times in a brief story. Several of the instances mentioned pertain to plot, but others function to emphasize the former and to provide aesthetic satisfaction. To use Poe's words, "by such means, with such care and skill, a picture is at length painted which leaves in the mind of him who contemplates it with a kindred art, a sense of the fullest satisfaction. The idea of the tale, its thesis, has been presented unblemished. . . . "[3] Here Poe is speaking specifically of "skilfully-constructed tales," and the complementary aspects of technique described are first to omit extraneous material and second to combine incidents, tone, and style to develop the "pre-established design." In this manner, form and "idea" become one. The thematic repetition and variation of incident in "The Tell-Tale Heart" offer one of the clearest examples of this architectural principle of Poe's at work.

Second, this slow-motion technique intensifies the subjectivity of "The Tell-Tale Heart" beyond that attained by mere use of a narrator. In the psychological triad of stimulus, internal response, and action, the first and third elements are slighted and the middle stage is given exaggerated attention.[4] In "The Tell-Tale Heart," stimulus in an objective sense scarcely exists at all. Only the man's eye motivates the murderer, and that almost wholly through his internal reaction to it. The action too, though decisive, is quickly over: "In an instant I dragged him to the floor, and pulled the heavy bed over him." In contrast, the intermediate, subjective experience is prolonged to a point where psychologically it is beyond objective measurement. At first the intervals receive conventional description—an "hour," or "many minutes"—but eventually such designations become meaningless and duration can be presented only in terms of the experience itself. Thus, in the conclusion of the story, the ringing in the madman's ears first is "fancied," then later becomes "distinct," then is discovered to be so "definite" that it is erroneously accorded external actuality, and finally grows to such obsessive proportions that it drives the criminal into an emotional and physical frenzy. Of the objective duration of these stages no information is given; the experience simply "continued" until "at length" the narrator "found" that its quality had changed.

Through such psychological handling of time Poe achieves in several of his most effective stories, including "The Tell-Tale Heart," two levels of chronological development which are at work simultaneously throughout the story. Typically, the action reaches its most intense point when the relation between the objective and subjective time sense falters or fails. At this point too the mental world of the subject is at its greatest danger of collapse. Thus we have the mental agony of the bound prisoner who loses all count of time as he alternately swoons and lives intensified existence while he observes the slowly descending pendulum. The narrator in "The Pit and the Pendulum" specifically refuses to accept responsibility for objective time-correlations: "There was another interval of insensibility; it was brief; for, upon again lapsing into life, there had been no perceptible descent in the pendulum. But it might have been long; for I knew there were demons who took note of my swoon, and who could have arrested the vibration at pleasure."[5]

These demons are his Inquisitional persecutors, but more subjective "demons" are at work in the timeless terror and fascination of the mariner whirled around the abyss in "The Descent into the Maelström," or the powerless waiting of Usher for days after he first hears his sister stirring within the tomb. In each instance the objective world has been reduced to the microcosm of an individual's experience; his time sense fades under the pressure of emotional stress and physical paralysis.

Even when not literally present, paralysis often may be regarded as symbolic in Poe's stories. In *The Narrative of Arthur Gordon Pym* (1838), Pym's terrifying dreams in the hold of the ship represent physical and mental paralysis: "Had a thousand lives hung upon the movement of a limb or the utterance of a syllable, I could have neither stirred nor spoken. . . . I felt that my powers of body and mind were fast leaving me."[6] Other examples are the "convolutions" of bonds about the narrator in "The Pit and the Pendulum," the death-grasp on the ring-bolt in "The Descent into the Maelström," the inaction of Roderick and (more literally) the catalepsy of Madeline Usher, and in part the supposed rationality of the madman in "The Tell-Tale Heart," which turns out to be subservience of his mental to his emotional nature. In most applications of the slow-motion technique in "The Tell-Tale Heart," three states of being are present concurrently: emotional tension, loss of mental grasp upon the actualities of the situation, and inability to act or to act deliberately. Often these conditions both invite and postpone catastrophe, with the effect of focusing attention upon the intervening experience.

In the two years following publication of "The Tell-Tale Heart," Poe extended this timeless paralysis to fantasies of hypnosis lasting beyond death. "Mesmeric Revelation" (1844) contains speculations about the relation between sensory experience and eternity. In "The Facts in the Case of M. Valdemar" (1845) the hypnotized subject is maintained for nearly seven months in a state of suspended "death" and undergoes instant dissolution when revived. His pleading for either life or death suggests that his internal condition had included awareness and suffering. Similarly the narrator in "The Tell-Tale Heart" records: "Oh God! what *could* I do? I foamed—I raved—I swore!" while all the time the police officers notice no foaming nor raving, for still they "chatted pleasantly, and smiled." His reaction is still essentially subjective, although he paces the room and grates his chair upon the boards above the beating heart. All these experiences move toward ultimate collapse, which is reached in "The Tell-Tale Heart" as it is for Usher and the hypnotized victims, while a last-moment reprieve is granted in "The Pit and the Pendulum" and "The Descent into the Maelström."

A second major theme in "The Tell-Tale Heart" is the murderer's psychological identification with the man he kills. Similar sensory details connect the two men. The vulture eye which the subject casts upon the narrator is duplicated in the "single dim ray" of the lantern that falls upon his own eye; like the unshuttered lantern, it is always one eye that is mentioned, never two. One man hears the creaking of the lantern hinge, the other the slipping of a finger upon the fastening. Both lie awake at midnight "hearkening to the death-watches in the wall." The loud yell of the murderer is echoed in the old man's shriek, which the narrator, as though with increasing clairvoyance, later tells the police was his own. Most of all the identity is implied in the key psychological occurrence in the story—the madman's mistaking his own heartbeat for that of his victim, both before and after the murder.

These two psychological themes—the indefinite extension of subjective time and the psychic merging of killer and killed—are linked closely together in the story. This is illustrated in the narrator's commentary after he has awakened the old man by an incautious sound and each waits for the other to move:

> Presently I heard a slight groan, and I knew it was the groan of mortal terror. It was not a groan of pain or of grief—oh, no! — it was the low stifled sound that arises from the bottom of the soul when overcharged with awe. I knew the sound well. Many a night, just at midnight, when all of the world slept, it has welled up from my own bosom, deepening, with its dreadful echo, the terrors that distracted me. I say I knew it well. I knew that he had been lying awake ever since the first slight noise, when he had turned in the bed. His fears had been ever since growing upon him. He had been trying to fancy them causeless, but could not. He had been saying to himself—"Is it nothing but the wind in the chimney—it is only a mouse crossing the floor," or "it is merely a cricket which has made a single chirp." Yes, he had been trying to comfort himself with these suppositions: but he had found all in vain.

Here the slow-motion technique is applied to both characters, with emphasis upon first their subjective experience and second the essential identity of that experience. The madman feels compelled to delay the murder until his subject is overcome by the same nameless fears that have possessed his own soul. The groan is an "echo" of these terrors within. The speaker has attempted a kind of catharsis by forcing his own inner horror to arise in his companion and then feeding his self-pity upon it. This pity cannot prevent the murder, which is a further attempt at exorcism. The final two sentences of the paragraph quoted explain why he believes that destruction is inevitable:

> *All in vain;* because Death, in approaching him, had stalked with his black shadow before him, and enveloped the victim. And it was the mournful influence of the unperceived shadow that caused him

to feel—although he neither saw nor heard—*to feel* the presence of my head within the room.

The significance of these sentences becomes clearer when we consider how strikingly the over-all effect of time-extension in "The Tell-Tale Heart" resembles that produced in Poe's "The Colloquy of Monos and Una," published two years earlier. In Monos's account of dying and passing into eternity, he prefaces his final experience with a sensory acuteness similar to that experienced by the narrator in "The Tell-Tale Heart." The senses were unusually active," Monos reports, "though eccentrically so. . . . " As the five senses fade in death, they are not utterly lost but merge into a sixth—of simple duration:

> Motion in the animal frame had fully ceased. No muscle quivered; no nerve thrilled; no artery throbbed. But there seems to have sprung up in the brain . . . a mental pendulous pulsation. . . . By its aid I measured the irregularities of the clock upon the mantel, and of the watches of the attendants. . . . And this—this keen, perfect, self-existing sentiment of *duration* . . . this sixth sense, upspringing from the ashes of the rest, was the first obvious and certain step of the intemporal soul upon the threshold of the temporal Eternity.[7]

Likewise the old man in "The Tell-Tale Heart" listens as though paralyzed, unable either to move or to hear anything that will dissolve his fears. This resembles Monos' sensory intensity and the cessation of "motion in the animal frame." Also subjective time is prolonged, becomes partially divorced from objective measurement, and dominates it. The most significant similarity comes in the conclusion of the experience. The old man does not know it but he is undergoing the same dissolution as Monos. He waits in vain for his fear to subside because actually it is "Death" whose shadow is approaching him, and "it was the mournful influence of that shadow that caused him to feel" his destroyer within the room. Like Monos, beyond his normal senses he has arrived at a "sixth sense," which is at first duration and then death.

But if the old man is nearing death so too must be the narrator, who has felt the same "mortal terror" in his own bosom. This similarity serves to unify the story. In Poe's tales, extreme sensitivity of the senses usually signalizes approaching death, as in the case of Monos and of Roderick Usher. This "over acuteness" in "The Tell-Tale Heart," however, pertains chiefly to the murderer, while death comes to the man with the "vulture eye." By making the narrator dramatize his feelings in the old man, Poe draws these two motifs together. We must remember, writes one commentator upon the story, "that the criminal sought his own death in that of his victim, and that he had in effect become the man who now lies dead."[8] Symbolically this is true. The resurgence of the beating heart shows that the horrors within himself, which the criminal attempted to identify with the old man and thus destroy, still live. In the death of the old man he sought to kill a part of himself, but his "demons" could not be exorcised through murder, for he himself is their destined victim.

From this point of view, the theme of "The Tell-Tale Heart" is self-destruction through extreme subjectivity marked paradoxically by both an excess of sensitivity and temporal solipsism. How seriously Poe could take this relativity of time and experience is evident in the poetic philosophy of his *Eureka* (1849). There time is extended almost infinitely into the life-cycle of the universe, but that cycle itself is only one heartbeat of God, who is the ultimate subjectivity. Romantically, indeed, Poe goes even further in the conclusion to *Eureka* and sees individual man becoming God, enclosing reality within himself, and acting as his own creative agent. In this state, distinction between subjective and objective fades: "the sense of individual identity will be gradually merged in the general consciousness."[9] Destruction then becomes self-destruction, the madman and his victim being aspects of the same universal identity. Death not only is self-willed but takes on some of the sanctity of creative and hence destructive Deity. The heartbeat of the red slayer and the slain merge in Poe's metaphysical speculations as well as in the denouement of a horror story.

This extreme subjectivity, moreover, leaves the ethical problem of "The Tell-Tale Heart" unresolved. In the opening paragraph of the story is foreshadowed an issue of good and evil connected with the speaker's madness: "I heard all things in the heaven and in the earth. I heard many things in hell. How, then, am I mad?" To be dramatically functional such an issue must be related to the murder. The only outward motivation for the murder is irritation at the vulture eye." It is the evil of the eye, not the old man (whom he "loved"), that the murderer can no longer live with, and to make sure that it is destroyed he will not kill the man while he is sleeping. What the "Evil Eye" represents that it so arouses the madman we do not know, but since he sees himself in his companion the result is self-knowledge. Vision becomes insight, the "Evil Eye" an evil "I," and the murdered man a victim sacrificed to a self-constituted deity. In this story, we have undeveloped hints of the self-abhorrence uncovered in "William Wilson" and "The Imp of the Perverse."

Poe also has left unresolved the story's ultimate degree of subjectivity. No objective setting is provided; so completely subjective is the narration that few or no points of alignment with the external world remain. From internal evidence, we assume the speaker to be mad, but whether his words constitute a defense before some criminal tribunal or the complete fantasy of a madman there is no way of ascertaining.[10] The difference, however, is not material, for the subjective experience, however come by, *is* the story. Psychologically, the lengthening concentration upon internal states of being has divorced the murderer first from normal chronology and finally from relationship with the "actual" world. The result, in Beach's words, is "disintegration of the psychological complex." The victim images himself as another and recoils from the vision. Seeing and seen eye become identical and must be destroyed.

From *Nineteenth-Century Fiction,* 19 (1965), 369-78.

1. "The Tell-Tale Heart," *Works,* ed. Clarence Edmund Stedman and George Edward Woodberry (New York, 1914). II, 70. Unless otherwise specified, all quotations from Poe are from this edition.

2. "Hawthorne's 'Tales'," *Works,* VII, 37.

3. "Twice-Told Tales," *Selected Writings of Edgar Allan Poe,* ed. Edward H. Davidson (Boston, 1956), p. 448.

4. Joseph Warren Beach in *The Twentieth-Century Novel* (New York, 1932), p. 407, describes a similar effect in stream-of-consciousness writing: "The subjective element becomes noticeable in fiction, as in everyday psychology, when an interval occurs between the stimulus to action and the resulting act." In extreme application of this technique, he declares, "there is a tendency to exhaust the content of the moment presented, there is *an infinite expansion of the moment,*" and he adds that the danger is that "there may come to pass a disintegration of the psychological complex, a divorce between motive and conduct" (p. 409). This is close to the state of Poe's narrator and murderer.

5. *Works,* I, 241-242.

6. *Works,* V, 38.

7. *Works,* I, 120-121.

8. Patrick F. Quinn, *The French Face of Edgar Poe* (Carbondale, Illinois, 1957), p. 236. Quinn makes this identity the theme of the story, without describing the full sensory patterns upon which it is based.

9. *Works,* IX, 164-169.

10. Despite lack of objective evidence, "The Tell-Tale Heart" bears much resemblance to a dream. The narrator acknowledges that the murdered man's shriek was such as occurs in dreams, and his memory of approaching the old man's bed upon eight successive midnights has the quality of a recurring nightmare. Poe frequently couples madness and dreaming, often with the variant "opium dreams," as in "Ligeia" and "The Fall of the House of Usher." "The Black Cat," a companion piece published the same year as "The Tell-Tale Heart" (1843), opens with an explicit denial of both madness and dreaming. The introductory paragraph of "Eleonora" (1842) runs the complete course of madness—dreams—death— good and evil: "Men have called me mad; but the question is not yet settled, whether madness is or is not the loftiest intelligence: whether much that is glorious, whether all that is profound, does not spring from disease of thought—from *moods* of mind exalted at the expense of the general intellect. They who dream by day are cognizant of many things which escape those who dream only by night. In their gray visions they obtain glimpses of eternity, and thrill, in awaking, to find that they have been upon the verge of the great secret. In snatches, they learn something of the wisdom which is of good, and more of the mere knowledge which is of evil" (*Works,* I, 96).

EDWARD H. DAVIDSON

The Meaning of "The Raven"

"THE RAVEN" is the fulfillment of these poems written in the twelve or thirteen years since the publication of the *Poems* of 1831. In it are the uses of pictorialism to suggest the inner workings of a disturbed consciousness and also the religious necessity, the drive of a consciousness toward understanding. We need not concern ourselves with the debate over Poe's sources and borrowings, whether the talking bird came from Dickens' *Barnaby Rudge* or whether the verse form was borrowed from Mrs. Browning's "Lady Geraldine's Courtship" (a debt which Poe may have silently acknowledged in his dedication of *The Raven* volume of poems "To Miss Elizabeth Barrett Barrett, of England"). These matters have been sufficiently discussed or even settled to allow us to pursue questions of the meaning of the poem and its relevance to Poe's poetic thought and practice.

A year or so after the poem was published in January 1845, Poe published "The Philosophy of Composition," an exposition of the poem-in-process which, in its own time as in after years, cast a little light and much confusion on the poem. We have had occasion to consider that essay in terms of Poe's theories of poetry and of art; here we might briefly mention that the essay was more an attempt to outline Poe's view of what poetry should be and should do than it was a forthright demonstration of how "The Raven" came to be. Thus the poem is made, in its after history, to conform to a preconceived philosophy of poetic composition—as if poems were written out of a schema or philosophy! Nonetheless, there are inevitable clues in the essay to what the poem was meant to be and how it came to have the form in which it was afterward resolved. Poe could not help admitting us to the inner rationale of how the poem was made.

The major clue which the essay provides is contained in a long sentence buried almost unobtrusively in the argument Poe was developing that works of art are constructed with their ends or climaxes always well in the artist's mind from the very beginning. We read, in part:

> I saw that I could make the first query propounded by the lover—
> the first query to which the Raven should reply "Nevermore"—that
> I could make this first query a commonplace one—the second less
> so—the third still less, and so on—until at length the lover, startled

from his original *nonchalance* by the melancholy character of the
word itself . . . propounds them half in superstition and half in that
species of despair which delights in self-torture—propounds
them . . . because he experiences a frenzied pleasure in so modeling
his questions as to receive from the *expected* "Nevermore" the
most delicious because the most intolerable of sorrow.

The clue leads us to an assumption that the student or protagonist
moves from the real world of dimension and time to a chaotic, fictive
world wherein nothing exists but the inner will and its morbid fantasies.
Let us first follow the narrative action of the poem.

The opening of the poem presents us with an action which has long
been under way. We are soon aware that much has occurred already:
the young man has lost his loved Lenore, and the shock of that loss is
not long past. Only by endurance or some act of will has he been able
to maintain his balance or sanity. It is in such a perilously maintained
balance, and in a room heavy with the remembrance of Lenore, that we
met him on the December night, a night which of itself is not unusual
in Virginia: a sleety storm and the gusty winds. There is nothing particularly unusual or *outré* about the student's room: as a titular goddess of
wisdom, the bust of Pallas reposes on a ledge above the outer door. The
student has sophisticated aesthetic tastes, for the windows are covered
with heavy, lustrous drapes, and cushions are placed about the room in
the style of the eighteen-forties. And the hour is midnight.

Into this special moment there is intruded a discordant rapping on
the outer door. The student's first impulse is, in Poe's explanation,
"adopting the half-fancy that it was the spirit of his mistress that
knocked." He throws open the door and finds no one outside; at this
moment, half of relief and half of disappointment, the young man
assumes the mood logical in such a situation, the mood of jocularity
that there should be any such disturbance at all, whether real or imaginary. He returns to his studies; then comes the rapping again. On this
occasion the student goes to the window and throws open the outer
lattice.

> . . . when, with many a flirt and flutter,
> In there stepped a stately Raven of the saintly days of yore;
> Not the least obeisance made he; not a minute stopped or stayed he;
> But, with mien of lord or lady, perched above my chamber door—
> Perched upon a bust of Pallas just above my chamber door. . .

At once, the jocular, humorous mood of the student is increased. Ex-
pecting, though not trusting, that the sound of knocking might have
been the spirit of the dead Lenore, the sudden presence of an ungainly
black bird is almost shattering. The lines quoted above are not how the

Raven looked as he came into the room but the way the Raven appeared to the student in his amazement. The student feels such surprise
to have a black embodiment of reality when he had hoped for a visita-
tion of a ghost that his mood of jocularity increases, quite naturally, to
one of hilarity. At once he takes the view that the Raven is a freak and
a joke and he makes sport of it. He propounds the first in a series of
three major questions: "Tell me what thy lordly name is on the Night's
Plutonian shore!" The pompous and inflated rhetoric of this query is
intended to underline the student's disbelief that the moment is real
and, concurrently, his normal impulse to ridicule that which seems so
very odd. The next stanza concludes this phase of the student's drama
through what Poe termed "superstition," or the doubt that what is
taking place should be taken at all seriously:

> For we cannot help agreeing that no living human being
> Ever yet was blessed with seeing bird above his chamber door—
> Bird or beast upon the sculptured bust above his chamber door,
> > With such name as "Nevermore."

This stanza also concludes the first half of the poem and marks a sharp
break in the action and the mood of the student.

Poe boasted in "The Philosophy of Composition" that his poem was
only 108 lines long; he was also mindful that the action of the poem
broke exactly at the end of line 54, wherein the mood of laughter and
freakish humor turned into a quite different temper. The second half of
the poem is action in disorder. The student quickly loses hold of himself and on reality: the bird's monotonous intoning of one senseless
word drives him into reverie, into the deepest recesses of his being into
which even the shattering impact of the death of Lenore had not
plunged him. From this point onward, both the questions which the
student asks and the one-word answer he receives are not "real" at all,
that is, they are not voiced; they are elements in an interior psychic
debate going forward in the young man's mind. What the Raven replies
is merely what the student himself wants to hear, must hear as more
and more he enters the dark, subliminal regions of his melancholy
which leads toward madness. The Raven as an object above the chamber door has ceased to exist; the poem becomes, in the latter fifty-four
lines, a dialogue of two voices or sides of the youthful protagonist who
asks those latter two questions and receives only his own interpretive
answer in the bird's one-word reply: "Is there . . . balm in Gilead?" (or,
is there any further release from anguish?) and "Tell this soul with
sorrow laden if . . . / It shall clasp a radiant maiden whom the angels
name Lenore?" (or, is there life after death?). These questions and their
inevitable answers mark the student's shift from a perilously maintained
balance of his faculties to their total disruption—a disruption which has

taken place not because the Raven has done or said anything but because the protagonist has put into those questions and into the answers
his most profound terror not only that Lenore is irrevocably lost in
death but that he himself exists in a state of death-in-life: the line
between human sanity and insanity, between life and death, is virtually
imperceptible. The Raven, the night storm, the bust of Pallas were
earlier conformable to the trusted routine of existence; they were facts
to be depended upon to have place and continuity. But under the
sudden impact of the strange and the terrible on the student's mind,
these objects were turned into the symbols of his maddened mind; they
have acted as part of the world which has driven the student from its
early rationalistic consciousness, then into the terror of the hitherto
concealed subconsciousness, and back again to consciousness, but now
it is a consciousness that the student is utterly maddened by his melancholy, and the terror is that he knows he has been driven to madness.
At the end, all of these signs and objects are frozen, just as the protagonists's mind is forever fixed in the inscrutable awareness that he will
never again have control over his mind and that what we call sanity is
only the veil that separates us from the total, and insane, mystery that
lies all around us:

> And the Raven, never flitting, still is sitting, *still* is sitting
> On the pallid bust of Pallas just above my chamber door;
> And the eyes have all the seeming of a demon's that is dreaming,
> And the lamp-light o'er him streaming
>   throws his shadow on the floor. . . .

The poem is, therefore, a set of stages in the process of self-
knowledge or the power of human consciousness to be aware not only
of its being but even of its non-being. Consciousness can be destroyed;
but the destruction can itself become a deeper self-consciousness. At
the beginning of the poem the young man is an innocent: even though
he has lost Lenore and presumably knows death, he is ignorant and
untried. Everything was outside; nothing had really happened to him.
But as the drama proceeds and the terror increases, the question of the
student's existence or Being itself dominates: he asks whether or not
there is any sensitivity or perception in life which is beyond the barriers
of ignorance we must endure in this existence. The replies, though in
the croaking voice of the Raven, are really from the innermost consciousness and even the subconsciousness of the student: his life is like
all life; there is a perpetual war between sentience within and insentient
chaos in the outer world; there is not even the comfortable illusion of
ultimate sentience in or beyond death. Being itself becomes an illusion,
a something we posit and live by in this existence in order better to
endure. Whatever order the world obtains is from within, is pure subjec-

tivism, is, as it were, imposed from within the "room" of the student. When this order is disrupted, the mind loses all hold on itself and on reality.

Once the mind loses that sense of selfhood, however illusory that sense may be, it is destroyed; the poem is a symbolic destruction of the mind by the impact of reality upon it. The poem is also raising the central question in nineteenth-century or romantic symbolism: what is the relation between reality and the mind's ideas about reality? There is nature, and there is mind, two polarities which may be separate and yet interact in the endless program of symbolic consciousness. This consciousness is a way of making the world intelligible, not from the mind alone or from a positing of the merely sensible world which makes impressions on the mind called "ideas," but from the action of the adjudicating power known as the imagination. In romantic formulations, such as those we have already seen in Coleridge, the imagination, whether primary or secondary, was a third or medial range of understanding, neither entirely of the mind nor of the sensible world. So long as the response between reality and imagination, on the one hand, and that between the mind and imagination, on the other, could be maintained, the romantic artist found expressive means of rendering ideas and experience in vivid, determinable ways: Hawthorne's red letter and Melville's whiteness of the whale are representative cases in point. But, once a rift appeared or a breakdown occurred at any moment in the process of the mind's finding expressive terms in the symbols which, consciously or not, mediated between reality and itself, then the symbolism became meaningless or was destroyed altogether.

Poe's "Raven" was a historic crisis in romantic artistic creation. In hardly more than a moment, wherein the Raven symbolized for the imagination its reach toward a further understanding of the illusion of reality and the painful awareness of nothing on the "other side" of reality, the symbolic perspective opened—as wide as Ishmael ever saw from the crow's nest or as deep as Hester Prynne ever saw into the abysses of sin and revenge. Then, all suddenly, the moment was gone; and Poe ended the poem, not because he believed that a poem should not much exceed a hundred lines but because his own symbolic imagination could go no further nor say anything more. The bird, the bust of Pallas, the light remained fixed in immobility. Poe termed it the "soul," but it was the imagination which

> . . . from out that shadow that lies floating on the floor
> Shall be lifted—nevermore!

The symbol had, for a moment, been able to transform reality. Then the sensible world remained resistant; reality was very real, and the shaping spirit withdrew from the final admission that it would have to remain content with conjuring the whole world according to its inner dream or allowing the imagination merely to report what outwardly it saw. Between the jocular first question, "Tell me what thy lordly name is on the Night's Plutonian shore," and the last question, the poetic imagination had caught fire and expressed the terror of loss of self and even of non-being. But the factual world remained fact and chaos; and the shaping spirit had nothing more to do. Poe admitted in "The Philosophy of Composition" that he wrote the climactic stanza first; if he did, then his penetration and his symbolic adventure were doomed from the outset.

Thus we can see the split in Poe's imaginative world: there were elements of reality, and there were faculties of the mind or imagination. Between them there ought to be a union or a point of coherence. At their best, his symbols are such mediations—the image of woman in "To Helen," the dramatic bird and its voice in "The Raven," the castle in "The Fall of the House of Usher," or the shifting reality in *Arthur Gordon Pym*. All the while he was erecting a theory to this fusion of mind and reality, the poetic enterprise was destroying any semblance of that unity, first, in the failure of the hypostatized "I" in the early poems to transform the world according to the necessities of the governing ego, and then in the inability to make a substitute "I," such as the student in "The Raven," itself proceed through the reordering of mind and reality. "The Raven" is a virtual admission of universal disparity: the imagination is lost in the shadow that lies upon the floor, while the inanimate objects, bird and bust, stare out in triumphant rigidity.

From *Poe: A Critical Study* (Cambridge, Mass.: The Belknap Press of Harvard Univ. Press, 1966), pp. 84-92.

KATHRYN M. HARRIS

Ironic Revenge in Poe's
"The Cask of Amontillado"

THE CASK OF AMONTILLADO has been less often read for itself than used to support theories about Poe's life, his psyche, or his narrative technique. It well illustrates his obsession with live burial and his use of sadism as a Gothic device,[1] and it meets exactly the criteria of unity and economy set out in his review of Hawthorne's *Twice-Told Tales.* But such readings separate theme and form, emphasizing one at the other's expense, and neglect the irony of Montresor's trowel, that symbol of brotherhood and instrument of death. This irony gives coherence to the images of the tale and to many of Montresor's apparently gratuitous, sadistic sarcasms—and suggest a motive for murder as well.[2]

From the beginning Montresor has a motive—or thinks he does: "The thousand injuries of Fortunato I had borne as best I could, but when he ventured upon insult I vowed revenge" (p. 167).[3] The chill grows as we progressively discover that Montresor, a connoisseur of the ironic, has a premeditated plan. Relying on Fortunato's envy and pride and his weakness for wine, he has arranged for his servants to desert for the holidays; he carries an ominous trowel beneath his cloak; the cave has been recently swept of old bones. Suddenly the plan is clear: entombment. And just as his revelation of the trowel at mid-point in their journey underground confirms the existence of a plan, its irony suggests his motive. When Montresor is surprised by a gesture of Fortunato's, Fortunato underscores his lack of comprehension; Fortunato is a freemason and Montresor is not:

> "Then you are not of the brotherhood."
> "How?"
> "You are not of the masons."
> "Yes, yes," I said. "Yes, yes."
> "You? Impossible! A mason?"
> "A mason," I replied.
> "A sign," he said, "a sign."
> "It is this," I answered producing from beneath the folds of my *requeuaire* a trowel.
> "You jest," he exclaimed, recoiling a few paces (pp. 171-172).

Fortunato's incredulity suggests that Montresor is a Catholic.

Earlier in the tale Montresor has gathered to himself several details that have religious, particularly Catholic, associations. The coat of arms of the house of Montresor with its vengeful motto, *"Nemo me impune lacessit,"* is more than a simple revenge motif. The circuitous device— "A huge human foot d'or, in a field of azure; the foot crushes a serpent rampant whose fangs are embedded in the heel" (p. 171)—is taken from the curse upon the serpent in Genesis 3:14. This is not an image of impartial revenge, but the traditional representation of the Church militant triumphing over the forces of evil in retribution for Adam's fall.[4]

"The Cask" is set at carnival time, a Catholic season, just before Lent, and the tale itself begins as a confession. The underground passages below the palazzo are literally "the catacombs of the Montresors" (p. 169), but the phrase also recalls the history of the early Church. The wine they seek, though its eucharistic significance is not elaborated, appropriately suggests through its non-existence the ironic perversion of Montresor's religious devotion.

Montresor's pun on "mason" is dramatized when he walls Fortunato behind eleven courses of carefully laid stone. He consistently describes his handiwork as "masonry" or "mason-work," and in the final paragraph, among the double-edged words *against* and *reerected* and the relics that may represent the Church, the word is surely symbolic: "Against the new masonry I re-erected the old rampart of bones" (p. 175). The story ends on a resoundingly Catholic note: *"In pace requiescat,"* the final words of the requiem mass.

Although the occasion for murder is as mysterious as ever, it is clear that the hostility between the two characters is worked out in terms of the Catholic-masonic opposition. This is not to say that Poe saw his tale as a morality play, a cataclysmic battle between Good and Evil, nor is it probable that Montresor is much more of a Catholic than Poe needed for the plot. Catholicism, like other aspects of medieval life, was for Poe a Gothic device used to intensify effect. Among Roderick Usher's favorite books are "a small octavo edition of the *Directorium Inquisitorum"* and "his chief delight," a "rare and curious book in quarto Gothic . . . the *Vigiliae Mortuorum Secundum Chorum Ecclesiae Maguntinae."*[5] The Inquisition is the source of horror in "The Pit and the Pendulum," and the Church and immurement are linked in "The Black Cat," whose protagonist conceals his wife's body in a wall "in the cellar—as the monks of the middle ages are recorded to have walled up their victims."[6]

Montresor's Catholicism—even if it is only nominal and melodramatic—is essential to the unity of the story. At the beginning Montresor gives us his two criteria for revenge: "A wrong," he says, "is unredressed when retribution overtakes its redresser. It is equally unredressed when the avenger fails to make himself felt as such to him who has done the wrong" (p. 167). The first requirement is fulfilled. No retribution seems to have overtaken Montresor. He does not speak from prison; his tone is never remorseful;[7] and in spite of the use in the story of religious trappings, there is no hint of divine retribution. But the second criterion is a loose end, a violation of narrative economy if Fortunato dies without understanding why.[8] Knowing Montresor is a Catholic, we, like Fortunato, can hear the irony of what have been seen as a villain's final sadistic sarcasms and understand the terms on which the revenge has been undertaken. By the time the first course is laid, the "intoxication of Fortunato had in a great measure worn off" (p. 174). He is sober enough to see Montresor's intent, to scream, to protest that he has seen the jest. He is sober enough to beg: *"For the love of God, Montresor!"* and to hear more than mere mockery in the reply. "Yes," I said, "for the love of God!" (p. 175). It is a declaration of motive, a triumphal boast, and the understanding silences Fortunato. The last stone is wedged into place.

The final line—*"In pace requiescat!"* —is not an expression of "sanctimonious contentment," a plea to be freed of guilt, or a sarcasm uttered as Montresor sees that Fortunato died without recognizing that his murder was an act of vengeance.[9] It is an appropriate ironic comment on the death of a mason, a sanctification of Montresor's private auto-da-fé.

Whether our failure to see the mason-Catholic conflict in the story has been the result of a modern preoccupation with mental aberration and "motiveless evil" or of Poe's failure to work out the conflict clearly, permitting his irony to give itself away more readily, "The Cask of Amontillado" is a more coherent tale than has been thought. Its details of honor are not merely decorative sadism but part of an ironic vengeance; and Montresor, whether his plan is evidence of sanity or madness, has what in Poe's world at least constitutes a motive for murder.

From *Studies in Short Fiction*, 6 (1969), 333-35.

1. Joseph Wood Krutch found the "simple sadism" of the story another of Poe's flights from reality to "neurotic delights" (*Edgar Allan Poe: A Study in Genius,* New York, 1926, p. 78). David M. Rein sees the story as a revenge fantasy with Fortunato standing for Mr. Allan (*Edgar A. Poe: The Inner Pattern,* New York, 1960, p. 42). Francis B. Dedmond takes the tale as psycho-drama: the avenger is Poe, the victim Thomas Dunn English, the cask Poe's libel suit against English (" 'The Cask of Amontillado' and the War of the Literati," *Modern Language Quarterly,* xv [1954] 137-146). Only recently has James W. Gargano defended the story as a work of art and "not just an ingenious Gothic exercise" (" 'The Cask of Amontillado': A Masquerade of Motive and Identity." *Studies in Short Fiction,* iv [1967], 119-126). For a fuller review of recent scholarship, see Gargano.

2. Montresor's apparent lack of motive has been exaggerated. Edward H. Davidson believes that in Montresor's narrative "The 'I' does not function as a mind; we never know what has made him hate Fortunato nor are we aware that he has even laid out any plan to effect his revenge" (*Edgar Allan Poe: A Critical*

Study, Cambridge, Mass., 1957, pp. 201-202). J. Rea maintains that Montresor's vengeance is merely an excuse used to conceal his motiveless perversity ("Poe's 'The Cask of Amontillado,' " *Studies in Short Fiction,* iv [1967], 55-69).

3. Page numbers in parentheses refer to *The Complete Works of Edgar Allan Poe,* The Virginia Edition, James A. Harrison, ed. (New York, 1902), vol. v.

4. See *Paradise Lost,* x, 179-190.

5. *The Complete Works,* Harrison, ed., II, 287.

6. *Ibid.* iv, 152.

7. Robert H. Fossum, however, sees a desire for peace of conscience, expressed in the final line, as Montresor's reason for telling the story after fifty years ("Poe's 'The Cask of Amontillado,' " *The Explicator,* xvii [1958], Item 16).

8. Believing that Fortunato dies unenlightened, Dorothy Norris Foote finds the irony of the story is at Montresor's expense (Poe's 'The Cask of Amontillado,' " *The Explicator,* xx [1961], Item 16).

9. The views, respectively, of Rein (p. 42), Fossum, and Foote.

SELECTED BIBLIOGRAPHY

Bibliography

Dameron, J. Lasley. *Edgar Allan Poe: A Checklist of Criticism 1942-1960.* Charlottesville, Va.: Bibliographical Society of the Univ. of Virginia, 1966.

Evans, May G. *Music and Edgar Allan Poe: A Bibliographical Study.* Baltimore: Johns Hopkins, 1939.

Heartmann, Charles F., and James R. Canny. *A Bibliography of First Printings of the Writings of Edgar Allan Poe.* Hattiesburg, Miss.: Brook Farm, 1940.

Hubbell, Jay B. "Poe." *Eight American Authors: A Review of Research and Criticism.* Ed. Floyd Stovall. New York: Norton, 1963.

Literary History of the United States. Ed. Robert E. Spiller, et al. New York: Macmillan, 1948, III, 689-96. *Bibliographical Supplement.* Ed. Richard M. Ludwig. New York: Macmillan, 1959, pp. 178-80.

Works

The Complete Works of Edgar Allan Poe. Ed. James A. Harrison, 17 vols. New York: Crowell, 1902.

The Poems of Edgar Allan Poe. Ed. Killis Campbell. Boston: Ginn, 1917.

Complete Poems and Stories of Edgar Allan Poe. Ed. Arthur H. Quinn and Edward H. O'Neill. 2 vols. New York: Knopf, 1946.

The Letters of Edgar Allan Poe. Ed. John W. Ostrom. 2 vols. Cambridge: Harvard Univ. Press, 1948.

Poe: Complete Poems. Ed. Richard Wilbur. New York: Dell, 1959.

Literary Criticism of Edgar Allan Poe. Ed. Robert L. Hough. Lincoln: Univ. of Nebraska Press, 1965.

The Poems of Edgar Allan Poe. Ed. Floyd Stovall, Charlottesville: The Univ. Press of Virginia, 1965.

Biography

Allen, Hervey. *Israfel: The Life and Times of Edgar Allan Poe.* 2 vols. New York: Doran, 1926.

Bonaparte, Marie. *The Life and Works of Edgar Allan Poe: A Psycho-Analytic Interpretation.* Trans. John Rodker. London: Imago Publishing, 1949.

Krutch, Joseph Wood. *Edgar Allan Poe: A Study in Genius.* New York: Knopf, 1926.

Quinn, Arthur Hobson. *Edgar Allan Poe: A Critical Biography.* New York: Appleton-Century-Crofts, 1941.

Wagenknecht, Edward. *Edgar Allan Poe: The Man Behind the Legend.* New York: Oxford Univ. Press, 1963.

Woodberry, George E. *The Life of Edgar Allan Poe, Personal and Literary.* 2 vols. Boston: Houghton, Mifflin, 1909.

Criticism

Abel, Darrel. "A Key to the House of Usher." *University of Toronto Quarterly,* 18 (1949), 176-85.
Allen, Gay Wilson. "Edgar Allan Poe." *American Prosody.* New York: American Book, 1935, pp. 56-85.
Alterton, Margaret. *Origins of Poe's Critical Theory.* Iowa City: Univ. of Iowa Press, 1925.
Bailey, James O. "What Happens in 'The Fall of the House of Usher'?" *American Literature,* 35 (1964), 445-61.
Baldwin, Summerfield. "The Aesthetic Theory of Edgar Poe." *Sewanee Review,* 27 (1918), 210-21.
Bandy, W. T. "New Light on Baudelaire and Poe." *Yale French Studies,* 10 (1953), 65-69.
Beebe, Maurice. "The Fall of the House of Pyncheon." *Nineteenth Century Fiction,* 11 (1956), 1-17.
Beebe, Maurice. "The Universe of Roderick Usher." *The Personalist,* 37 (1956), 147-60.
Bezanson, Walter E. "The Troubled Sleep of Arthur Gordon Pym." *Essays in Literary History, Presented to J. Milton French.* Ed. R. Kirk and C. F. Main. New Brunswick, N.J.: Rutgers Univ. Press, 1960, pp. 149-75.
Blair, Walter. "Poe's Conception of Incident and Tone in the Tale." *Modern Philology,* 41 (1944), 228-40.
Blankenship, Russell. "The Scope of Poe's Art." *American Literature as an Expression of the National Mind.* New York: Holt, 1958, pp. 214-18.
Braddy, Haldeen. *The Glorious Incense: The Fulfillment of Edgar Allan Poe.* New Brunswick, N.J.: Scarecrow Press, 1953.
Brownell, W. C. *American Prose Masters: Cooper—Hawthorne—Emerson—Poe—Lowell—Henry James.* New York: Scribner's, 1909.
Campbell, Killis. *The Mind of Poe and Other Studies.* Cambridge, Mass.: Harvard Univ. Press, 1933.
Canby, Henry Seidel. *Classic Americans.* New York: Russell & Russell, 1959.
Carlson, Eric W., ed. *The Recognition of Edgar Allan Poe: Selected Criticism Since 1829.* Ann Arbor: Univ. of Michigan Press, 1966.
Carlson, Eric W. "Symbol and Sense in Poe's 'Ulalume.'" *American Literature,* 35 (1963), 22-37.
Covici, Pascal, Jr. "Toward a Reading of Poe's *Narrative of A. Gordon Pym.*" *Mississippi Quarterly,* 21 (1968), 111-18.
Cowley, Malcolm. "The Edgar Allan Poe Tradition." *Outlook,* 149 (1928), 497-99, 511.
Cunliffe, Marcus. "The Dubious Talents of Poe." *The Literature of the United States.* Baltimore: Penguin Books, 1970, pp. 70-79.
Damerson, J. Lasley. "Poe at Mid-Century: Anglo-American Criticism, 1928-1960." *Ball State University Forum,* 8 (1967), 36-44.
Daniel, Robert. "Poe's Detective God." *Furioso* (Summer 1951), 45-54.
Fagin, N. Bryllion. *The Histrionic Mr. Poe.* Baltimore: Johns Hopkins, 1949.
Gargano, James W. "'The Black Cat': Perverseness Reconsidered." *Texas Studies in Literature and Language,* 2 (1960), 172-78.
Gargano, James W. "Poe's 'Ligeia': Dream and Destruction." *College English,* 23 (1962), 337-42.
Garrison, Joseph M., Jr. "The Function of Terror in the Work of Edgar Allan Poe." *American Quarterly,* 18 (1966), 136-50.
Hofrichter, Laura. "From Poe to Kafka." *Univ. of Toronto Quarterly,* 29 (1960), 405-19.

Hubbell, Jay B. "The Literary Apprenticeship of Edgar Allan Poe." *Southern Literary Journal,* 2 (1969), 99-105.

Hubbell, Jay B. "Poe and the Southern Literary Tradition." *Texas Studies in Literature and Language,* 2 (1960), 151-71; rev. as "Edgar Allan Poe and the South," in Hubbell, *South and Southwest,* Durham: Duke Univ. Press, 1965.

Hungerford, E. "Poe and Phrenology." *American Literature,* 2 (1930), 209-31.

Jacobs, Robert D. "Poe and the Agrarian Critics." *Hopkins Review,* 5 (1952), 43-54.

Jacobs, Robert D. "Poe's Earthly Paradise." *American Quarterly,* 12 (1960), 404-13.

Jones, Howard M. "Poe, 'The Raven,' and the Anonymous Young Man." *Western Humanities Review,* 9 (1955), 127-38.

Kelly, George. "Poe's Theory of Beauty." *American Literature,* 27 (1956), 521-36.

Lafleur, L. J. "Edgar Allan Poe as Philosopher." *The Personalist,* 22 (1941), 401-5.

Laser, Marvin. "The Growth and Structure of Poe's Concept of Beauty." *Journal of English Literature History,* 15 (1948), 69-84.

Lawrence, D. H. " 'Ligeia': Poe's Love Story." *Studies in Classic American Literature.* Garden City, N.Y.: Doubleday, 1951, pp. 78-85.

Levin, Harry. *The Power of Blackness.* New York: Knopf, 1958.

Lind, S. E. "Poe and Mesmerism." *PMLA,* 62 (1947), 1077-94.

Lovecraft, Howard P. "Edgar Allan Poe." *The Supernatural Horror in Literature.* New York: B. Abramson, 1945, pp. 52-59.

Mabbott, Thomas O. "Poe's 'Ulalume.' " *Explicator,* 1, No. 4 (1943), Item 25.

Maddison, Carol H. "Poe's *Eureka.*" *Texas Studies in Literature and Language,* 2 (1960), 350-67.

Marchand, Ernest. "Poe As Social Critic." *American Literature,* 6 (1934), 28-43.

Marks, E. R. "Poe As Literary Theorist: A Reappraisal." *American Literature,* 33 (1961), 296-306.

Matthiessen, F. O. "Poe." *Sewanee Review,* 54 (1946), 175-205.

Miller, James E., Jr. "Ulalume Resurrected." *Philological Quarterly,* 34 (1955), 197-205.

Mooney, Stephen L. "The Comic in Poe's Fiction." *American Literature,* 33 (1962), 433-41.

Mooney, Stephen L. "Poe's Gothic Waste Land." *Sewanee Review,* 70 (1962), 261-83.

Moss, Sidney P. "*Arthur Gordon Pym,* or the Fallacy of Thematic Interpretation." *University Review,* 33 (1967), 299-306.

Moss, Sidney P. *Poe's Literary Battles.* Durham: Duke Univ. Press, 1963.

Moss, Sidney P. *Poe's Major Crisis: His Libel Suit and New York's Literary World.* Durham: Duke Univ. Press, 1970.

O'Donnell, Charles R. "From Earth to Ether: Poe's Flight into Space." *PMLA,* 77 (1962), 85-91.

Parks, Edd W. *Edgar Allan Poe as Literary Critic.* Athens: Univ. of Georgia Press, 1964.

Pollin, Burton R. *Discoveries in Poe.* Notre Dame: Univ. of Notre Dame Press, 1970.

Pritchard, John Paul. *Criticism in America.* Norman: Univ. of Oklahoma Press, 1956.

Quinn, A. H. "Beauty and the Supernatural." *The Literature of the American People.* New York: Appleton-Century-Crofts, 1951, pp. 292-307.

Quinn, Patrick F. *The French Face of Edgar Poe.* Carbondale: Southern Illinois Univ. Press, 1957.

Rans, Geoffrey. *Edgar Allan Poe.* Edinburgh: Oliver & Boyd, 1965.

Shaw, George Bernard. "Edgar Allan Poe." *Nation,* 4 (1909), 601-2; rpt. in *Works,* vol. 29, London: Constable, 1930, 231-38.

Snell, George. "First of the New Critics." *Quarterly Review of Literature,* 2 (1945), 330-40.

Stockton, Eric W. "Celestial Inferno: Poe's 'The City in the Sea.'" *Tennessee Studies in Literature,* 8 (1963), 99-106.

Stovall, Floyd. *Edgar Poe the Poet: Essays New and Old on the Man and His Work.* Charlottesville: Univ. Press of Virginia, 1969.

Stovall, Floyd. "The Conscious Art of Edgar Allan Poe." *College English,* 24 (1963), 417-21.

Stroupe, John H. "Poe's Imaginary Voyage: Pym as Hero." *Studies in Short Fiction,* 4 (1967), 315-21.

Tate, Allen. "The Angelic Imagination." *Kenyon Review,* 14 (1952), 455-75.

Vanderbilt, Kermit. "Art and Nature in 'The Masque of the Red Death.'" *Nineteenth-Century Fiction,* 22 (1968), 379-89.

Walsh, John. *Poe The Detective: The Curious Circumstances Behind "The Mystery of Marie Roget."* New Brunswick: Rutgers Univ. Press, 1967.

Wilber, Richard. "Edgar Allan Poe." *Major Writers of America,* ed. P. G. E. Miller. New York: Harcourt, Brace & World, 1962. Vol. 1, 369-82.

Williams, William Carlos. "Edgar Allan Poe." *In the American Grain.* Norfolk, Conn.: New Directions, 1925, 1956, pp. 216-33.

Williams, Paul O. "A Reading of Poe's 'The Bells.'" *Poe Newsletter,* 1 (1968), 24-25.

Wilson, Edmund. "Poe at Home and Abroad." *New Republic,* 49 (1926), 77-80.

Winters, Yvor. "Edgar Allan Poe: A Crisis in the History of American Obscurantism." *American Literature,* 8 (1937), 379-401.

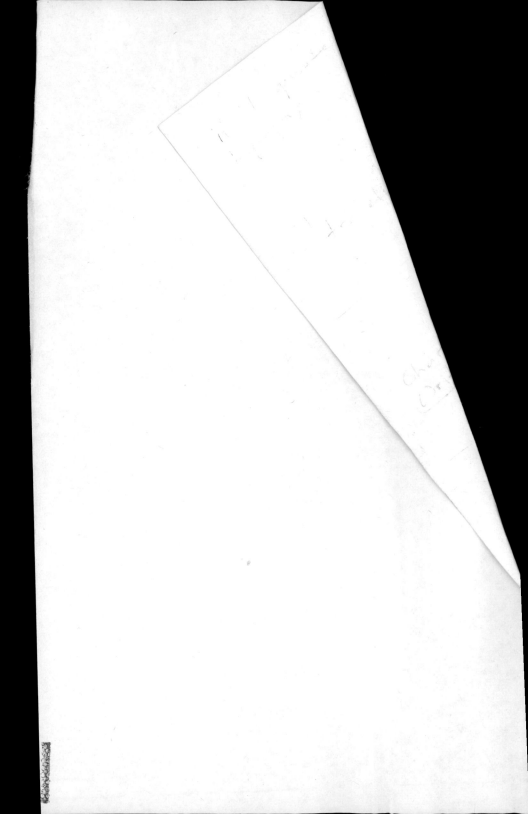